Casseroles, One-Dish Meals
and More

Publications International Ltd.

Favorite Brand Name Recipes at www.fbnr.com

Microwave Cooking: Microwave ovens vary in wattage. Use the cooking times as guidelines and check for doneness before adding more time.

Preparation/Cooking Times: Preparation times are based on the approximate amount of time required to assemble the recipe before cooking, baking, chilling or serving. These times include preparation steps such as measuring, chopping and mixing. The fact that some preparations and cooking can be done simultaneously is taken into account. Preparation of optional ingredients and serving suggestions is not included.

Table of CONTENTS

One casserole.
One skillet.
One slow cooker.

ONE EASY AND DELICIOUS MEAL

Getting dinner on the table doesn't get much simpler than combining ingredients in one dish and letting the stove or slow cooker do the work. Not only is the meal you set before your family easy for you to prepare, but it also requires only minimal cleanup—and most importantly, it's a meal you know they'll all love.

Since 1940, Campbell's® Kitchen has helped feed America's families, not just by creating delicious soups, broths and other foods, but also by offering ways to use those foods in family-pleasing recipes. And one of the most popular ways cooks use Campbell's foods is as a key ingredient in America's favorite home-cooked dinners: one-dish meals.

Campbell's Kitchen is proud to bring you our latest cookbook, *Casseroles, One-Dish and More*. Whether you're looking for new recipes for slow cooker dinners, skillet meals or oven-baked casseroles, or your old favorites, you'll find them all in this book. We hope this finds a permanent home in your kitchen and that we continue to inspire you to cook the meals your family loves.

WHAT'S THE DIFFERENCE?

Throughout this book, we'll give you tips and recipes on casseroles, one-dish meals, skillet dinners and more. It will help to get our terminology straight: For example, we're often asked the difference between a casserole and a "bake" or one-dish oven-baked meal. A casserole is a

deep, round or oval, ovenproof baking dish made from glass, ceramic or other heat-resistant material. Casseroles usually have two handles and tight-fitting lids. "Casserole" also refers to the food that's baked in a casserole.

A baking dish is a shallow, glass or ceramic, heat-resistant dish used for baking main dishes, side dishes and desserts. Baking dishes are available in various shapes and sizes and often come with lids for easy reheating and storage. Popular sizes include 13×9×2-inch dishes, and 8- and 9-inch pans.

TOP OFF YOUR CASSEROLE

Casseroles taste best when they're topped off. Try these toppings:

✔ Pepperidge Farm® croutons: Choose from a variety of flavors.

✔ Homemade breadcrumbs: A great way to use up day-old bread is to make your own breadcrumbs. For dry breadcrumbs, preheat your oven to 300°F. Place a single layer of bread slices on a baking sheet; bake 5 to 8 minutes or until they're completely dry and lightly browned. Cool completely. Process in a food processor or crush or crumble in a plastic food storage bag until crumbs are very fine. Season with black pepper, garlic powder, dried herbs or spices or grated cheese, as desired. To make fresh breadcrumbs, process untoasted bread in a food processor and process until crumbs are fine. Season as desired.

✔ Toasted almonds, pine nuts or walnuts. You'll love the nutty flavor they add to your dish.

✔ Dried fruits or vegetables: Try some dried cranberries, raisins, even cherries, or maybe some

CASSEROLE CAPACITY

Not sure your casserole is the right size for the recipe? Square and rectangular casseroles are commonly measured in inches. If the dimensions aren't marked on the bottom of the casserole, use a ruler to measure on top from the inside of one edge to the inside of the opposite edge.

Round and oval casseroles are usually measured in cups or quarts. If you're unsure about the capacity of a casserole, one way to find out its volume is to pour 1-cup measures of water into the dish until it's full. The amount of water in the dish is equivalent to the size of the casserole. Here's a guide for converting cups to quarts:

4 cups = 1 quart
6 cups = 1^1/$_2$ quarts
8 cups = 2 quarts
10 cups = 2^1/$_2$ quarts
12 cups = 3 quarts
14 cups = 3^1/$_2$ quarts

chopped bell peppers or shredded carrots.

✔ Cheese: Shredded varieties, including Cheddar, Swiss and mozzarella, will top off your dish with lots of flavor.

✔ Crushed chips, cereals or French fried onions: Crushed or crumbled potato chips, tortilla chips, French fried onions and unsweetened cereals can add a flavorful crunch to your favorite dish.

LOOKING FOR MORE CASSEROLE CONVENIENCE?

Slightly undercook pasta or rice before adding it to a casserole or other baked one-dish meal. You want

it almost tender but still somewhat chewy. The pasta or rice will finish cooking while the casserole bakes.

How can you make one-dish meals even more convenient? By having prepared, cooked chicken on hand in the freezer. Buy boneless chicken breasts, cut them into bite-size pieces and stir-fry in a little vegetable or olive oil in a skillet over medium heat until they're no longer pink in the center. Drain off the fat, and package them in 1- and 2-cup amounts in sealable plastic freezer bags. Freeze. Thaw in the refrigerator or in the microwave, and use according to recipe directions.

SLOW-COOKER KNOW-HOW

A few things to remember when breaking out your slow cooker:

✔ For easy cleanup, spray the crock with nonstick cooking spray before adding the food. Or, try the new slow cooker liner bags. (To clean your slow cooker, follow the manufacturer's instructions.)

✔ Slow cookers work best when they're two-thirds to three-quarters full. That's because most slow cookers' heating units are coiled inside the outer walls that surround the crockery insert rather than on the bottom of the crock.

✔ Keep a lid on it! The slow cooker can take as long as

20 minutes to regain the heat lost when the cover is removed. If the recipe calls for stirring or checking the dish near the end of the cooking time, replace the lid as quickly as you can. Otherwise, unless the recipe instructs you to remove the lid, don't, or food will take much longer to cook.

✔ Believe it or not, some vegetables can take longer to cook than meat. Pay careful attention to the recipe instructions so you're sure to cut vegetables in the proper size and add them to the slow cooker in the correct order. By the way, frozen vegetables should be thawed before adding to the slow cooker; frozen foods lower the temperature inside the cooker and can play havoc with cooking times.

✔ Slow cookers retain moisture, so you don't have to begin with as much liquid. Actually, much of the time, you don't have to begin with any; any flavorful liquid, such as Swanson® Broth, Campbell's® Soup, or Pace® Salsa or Picante Sauce, can be used and become an excellent sauce or gravy for the meal.

SAFE SLOW COOKING

✔ If you do any advance preparation, such as trimming meat or cutting vegetables, make sure you keep the food covered and

refrigerated until you're ready to add them to the cooker. Store uncooked meats and vegetables separately. After you've prepared raw meat, poultry or fish, remember to wash your cutting board, utensils, countertops, sink and hands with hot soapy water. (Many cooks have plastic cutting boards that they use only for meat preparation so they can wash and sterilize
them in the dishwasher after use.)

✓ Once your dish is cooked, serve it immediately. After serving, transfer food to a clean container, and cover and refrigerate it immediately. Do not reheat leftovers in the slow cooker. Use a microwave oven, on top of the stove or the oven for reheating.

SKILLET SAVVY

✓ What's the best skillet to use for a skillet dinner? Also called frying pans, skillets are round, shallow pans with straight or sloping sides and long handles. They come in a wide range of sizes. Experts generally consider the best choice to be enameled cast iron, or heavy stainless steel with aluminum bottoms. Most cooks find the 8-, 10- and 12-inch sizes to be the most useful, but follow your recipe guidelines.

Use leftover foods, such as cooked vegetables, pasta, rice, chicken and beef. They see new life as ingredients in skillet dinners.

STOCK UP

Keeping your pantry stocked with staples means a quick and easy one-dish meal is always at hand. If you follow this guide, you'll almost always be able to put together many of the recipes in this book.

PANTRY:

Beans, canned and dried

Breadcrumbs

Campbell's® soups (including regular and 98% Fat free and broths), especially cream soups

Canned fish, tuna, and salmon

Chunky™ soup and chili varieties

Flour, all-purpose and whole-wheat

Fruits, canned

Herbs and spices, dried and fresh

Nonstick cooking spray

Oils, vegetable and olive

Onions

Pace® Salsa and Picante Sauces

Pasta, in a variety of shapes and sizes; egg noodles

Pepperidge Farm® assorted crackers, snacks and cookies

Potatoes, white and sweet, instant mashed

Rice, quick-cooking and long-grain, white and brown

Pepperidge Farm® Goldfish®

Prego® Italian and Meat Sauces and other sauces including barbecue, ketchup, soy and teriyaki

Swanson® Broths, chicken, beef and vegetable varieties

Tomatoes, canned

Vegetables, canned

Vinegar, white, balsamic and flavored

V8® and V8 Splash® Juices

FREEZER AND REFRIGERATOR:

Boneless, skinless chicken breasts

Canned breadsticks, rolls, pizza dough, biscuits

Cheeses, shredded

Fish fillets

Lean beef, ground or roast

Dairy products, milk, yogurt, sour cream

Pepperidge Farm® Puff Pastry

Vegetables and fruits, frozen and fresh

Comfort of BEEF

FAMILY FAVORITE COMFORT
MEALS MADE WITH BEEF

Beef Bourguignonne

MAKES: **6 SERVINGS**

START TO FINISH:
*8 to 9 hours,
10 minutes*

Prep: *10 minutes*

Cook: *8 to 9 hours*

1 can (10¾ ounces) Campbell's® Condensed Golden Mushroom Soup
1 cup Burgundy **or** other dry red wine
2 cloves garlic, minced
1 teaspoon dried thyme leaves, crushed
2 cups small button mushrooms (about 6 ounces)
2 cups fresh **or** frozen whole baby carrots
1 cup frozen small whole onions
1½ pounds beef top round steak, 1½-inch thick, cut into 1-inch pieces

1. Stir the soup, wine, garlic, thyme, mushrooms, carrots, onions and beef in a 3½-quart slow cooker.

2. Cover and cook on LOW for 8 to 9 hours* or until the meat is fork-tender.

*Or on HIGH for 4 to 5 hours

Hearty Beef and Vegetable Soup

MAKES: **8 SERVINGS**

START TO FINISH:
1 hour, 10 minutes

Prep: *10 minutes*
Cook: *1 hour*

2 tablespoons vegetable oil
2 pounds boneless beef chuck steak (1½-inch thick), cut into 1-inch pieces
2 cans (10½ ounces **each**) Campbell's® Condensed Beef Broth
2 cups water
1 tablespoon chili powder
1 teaspoon paprika
⅛ teaspoon ground black pepper
1 large onion, chopped (about 1 cup)
8 small turnips (about 1½ pounds), peeled
4 ears frozen corn on the cob, thawed and cut in half

1. Heat the oil in a 6-quart saucepot over medium-high heat. Add the beef in 2 batches and cook until it's well browned on all sides, stirring often. Remove the beef with a slotted spoon and set it aside.

2. Stir the broth, water, chili powder, paprika, black pepper, onion and turnips into the saucepot. Heat to a boil. Return the beef to the pot and reduce the heat to low. Cover and cook for 25 minutes.

3. Add the corn. Cover and cook for 20 minutes more or until the meat and vegetables are fork-tender. Stir the soup occasionally while cooking.

Beef Taco Bake

MAKES: **4 SERVINGS**

START TO FINISH:
40 minutes

Prep: *10 minutes*
Bake: *30 minutes*

1 pound ground beef
1 can (10¾ ounces) Campbell's® Condensed Tomato Soup
1 cup Pace® Chunky Salsa **or** Picante Sauce
½ cup milk
6 (8-inch) flour tortillas **or** 8 (6-inch) corn tortillas, cut into 1-inch pieces
1 cup shredded Cheddar cheese (4 ounces)

1. Cook the beef in a 10-inch skillet over medium-high heat until the beef is well browned, stirring frequently to break up meat. Pour off any fat.

2. Stir the soup, salsa, milk, tortillas and ½ **cup** of the cheese into the skillet. Spoon the mixture into a 12×8×2-inch shallow baking dish. Cover the dish with foil.

3. Bake at 400°F. for 30 minutes or until hot. Sprinkle with remaining cheese.

Herbed Beef & Vegetable Skillet

START TO FINISH:
30 minutes

Prep: *10 minutes*

Cook: *20 minutes*

MAKES: **4 SERVINGS**

2 tablespoons vegetable **or** canola oil

1 pound boneless beef sirloin **or** top round steak, ¾-inch thick, cut into thin strips

3 medium carrots, sliced thin diagonally (about 1½ cups)

1 medium onion, chopped (about ½ cup)

2 cloves garlic, minced

½ teaspoon dried thyme leaves, crushed

1 can (10¾ ounces) Campbell's® Condensed Golden Mushroom Soup

¼ cup water

2 teaspoons Worcestershire sauce

⅛ teaspoon ground black pepper

Hot cooked noodles

1. Heat **1 tablespoon** of the oil in a 12-inch skillet over medium-high heat. Add the beef and cook and stir until it's well browned. Remove beef with a slotted spoon and set aside.

2. Reduce the heat to medium and add the remaining oil. Add the carrots, onion, garlic and thyme. Cook and stir until the vegetables are tender-crisp.

3. Stir the soup, water, Worcestershire and black pepper into the skillet. Heat to a boil. Return the beef to the skillet. Cook until mixture is hot and bubbling. Serve over the noodles.

Beef Stir-Fry

MAKES: **4 SERVINGS**

START TO FINISH:
30 minutes

Prep: *10 minutes*
Cook: *20 minutes*

- 2 tablespoons cornstarch
- 1 can (10½ ounces) Campbell's® Condensed Beef Broth
- 2 tablespoons soy sauce
- 2 tablespoons vegetable oil
- 1 pound boneless beef sirloin **or** top round steak, ¾-inch thick, cut into thin strips
- 3 cups cut-up vegetables*
- ¼ teaspoon garlic powder **or** 1 clove garlic, minced

  Hot cooked rice

1. Stir the cornstarch, broth and soy in a small bowl. Set the mixture aside.

2. Heat the oil in a 10-inch skillet over medium-high heat. Add the beef and stir-fry until well browned. Push beef to one side of the skillet.

3. Add the vegetables and garlic powder and stir-fry until tender-crisp.

4. Stir the cornstarch mixture and stir it into the skillet. Cook and stir until the mixture boils and thickens. Serve over the rice.

Use broccoli flowerets, sliced carrots and green or red pepper strips.

Southwest Beef Skillet Dinner

MAKES: **4 SERVINGS**

START TO FINISH:
1 hour, 30 minutes

Prep: *15 minutes*

Cook: *1 hour,
15 minutes*

1 pound boneless beef sirloin **or** top round
   steak, cut in thin strips
2 tablespoons all-purpose flour
2 tablespoons vegetable oil
¾ cup chopped onion
2 cloves garlic, minced
1 can (10¾ ounces) Campbell's® Condensed
   Creamy Ranchero Tomato Soup
1 cup water
¼ teaspoon chili powder
1 cup frozen whole kernel corn
   Hot cooked cholesterol-free wide
   noodle-style pasta

1. Coat the beef with the flour.

2. Heat **1 tablespoon** of the oil in a 4-quart saucepan over medium-high heat. Add the beef and cook until it's well browned, stirring often. Remove the beef with a slotted spoon and set aside.

3. Reduce the heat to medium and add the remaining oil. Add the onion and garlic. Cook for 1 minute.

4. Stir the soup, water and chili powder into the saucepan. Heat to a boil. Return the beef to the saucepan and reduce the heat to low. Cover and cook for 1 hour.

5. Stir in the corn. Serve over the pasta.

Cheeseburger Pasta

MAKES: **4 SERVINGS**

START TO FINISH:
20 minutes

Prep/Cook: *20 minutes*

1   **pound ground beef**
1   **can (10¾ ounces) Campbell's® Condensed Cheddar Cheese Soup**
1   **can (10½ ounces) Campbell's® Condensed Beef Broth**
1½   **cups water**
½   **cup ketchup**
2   **cups uncooked shell-shaped (medium shells) pasta**

1. Cook the beef in a 10-inch skillet over medium-high heat until the beef is well browned, stirring frequently to break up meat. Pour off any fat.

2. Stir the soup, broth, water, ketchup and pasta into the skillet. Heat to a boil. Reduce the heat to medium. Cook for 10 minutes or until the pasta is tender but still firm, stirring often.

Easy Beef & Pasta

MAKES: **4 SERVINGS**

- 1 tablespoon vegetable oil
- 1 pound boneless beef sirloin **or** top round steak, ¾-inch thick, cut into thin strips
- 1 can (10¾ ounces) Campbell's® Condensed Tomato Soup
- ½ cup water
- 1 bag (about 16 ounces) frozen vegetable and pasta blend

START TO FINISH:
20 minutes

Prep: *5 minutes*
Cook: *15 minutes*

1. Heat the oil in a 10-inch skillet over medium-high heat. Add the beef and cook until it's well browned, stirring often.

2. Stir the soup, water and vegetable pasta blend into the skillet. Heat to a boil. Reduce the heat to low. Cover and cook for 5 minutes or until the pasta is tender but still firm.

Beef Stroganoff

MAKES: **4 SERVINGS**

1 pound boneless beef sirloin **or** top round steak, ¾-inch thick
  Cracked black pepper
1 tablespoon vegetable oil
1 medium onion, finely chopped (about ½ cup)
1 can (10¾ ounces) Campbell's® Condensed Cream of Mushroom Soup (Regular **or** 98% Fat Free)
½ cup water
¼ cup dry sherry (optional)
1 tablespoon tomato paste
¼ cup plain yogurt
  Hot cooked egg noodles
  Chopped fresh parsley

1. Cut the beef into 2-inch pieces. Coat the beef with the black pepper.

2. Heat the oil in a 10-inch skillet over medium-high heat. Add the beef and cook until it's well browned on all sides, stirring often. Remove the beef with a slotted spoon and set it aside.

3. Reduce the heat to medium. Add the onion. Cook and stir until the onion is tender.

4. Stir the soup, water, sherry, if desired, and tomato paste into the skillet. Heat to a boil. Return the beef to the skillet and heat through. Remove from the heat. Stir in the yogurt. Serve over the noodles and sprinkle with the parsley.

Garlic Mashed Potatoes & Beef Bake

START TO FINISH:
35 minutes

Prep: *5 minutes*
Cook/Bake: *30 minutes*

MAKES: **4 SERVINGS**

Time-Saving Tip:
To thaw vegetables,
microwave on HIGH
for 3 minutes.

1 pound ground beef **or** ground turkey
1 can (10¾ ounces) Campbell's® Condensed
    Cream of Mushroom with Roasted Garlic
    Soup
1 tablespoon Worcestershire sauce
1 bag (16 ounces) frozen vegetables
    combination (broccoli, cauliflower,
    carrots), thawed
2 cups water
3 tablespoons butter
¾ cup milk
2 cups instant potato flakes **or** buds

1. Cook the beef in a 10-inch skillet over
medium-high heat until the beef is well browned,
stirring frequently to break up meat. Pour off any
fat.

2. Stir the beef, ½ **can** soup, Worcestershire and
vegetables in a 12×8×2-inch shallow baking dish.

3. Heat the water, butter and remaining soup in a
2-quart saucepan over high heat to a boil. Remove
from the heat. Stir in the milk. Slowly stir in the
potatoes. Spoon potatoes over the beef mixture.

4. Bake at 400°F. for 20 minutes or until hot.

3-Cheese Baked Bolognese with Mostaccioli

MAKES: **6 SERVINGS**

START TO FINISH:
40 minutes

Prep/Cook: *20 minutes*

Bake: *20 minutes*

- 1 **pound ground beef**
- 2 **cloves garlic, minced**
- 1 **medium zucchini, cut in half lengthwise and sliced (about 1½ cups)**
- 1 **jar (1 pound 10 ounces) Prego® Traditional Italian Sauce or 1 jar (1 pound 9 ounces) Prego® Organic Tomato & Basil Italian Sauce**
- 1 **package (16 ounces) medium tube-shaped pasta (mostaccioli or ziti), cooked and drained**
- 1½ **cups shredded mozzarella cheese (6 ounces)**
- 1 **cup ricotta cheese**
- ¼ **cup grated Parmesan cheese**

Make Ahead Tip:
Prepare recipe through step 2. Cover the dish with foil. Refrigerate up to 8 hours. To heat, bake covered, at 400°F. for 30 minutes or until hot and bubbly.

1. Cook the beef and garlic in a 12-inch skillet over medium-high heat until the beef is well browned, stirring frequently to break up meat. Pour off any fat. Add the zucchini and cook until the zucchini is tender. Stir in the Italian sauce. Remove from the heat.

2. Stir the beef mixture, pasta, ½ **cup** of the mozzarella cheese, ricotta cheese and the Parmesan cheese in a 13×9×2-inch shallow baking dish. Sprinkle with the remaining mozzarella cheese.

3. Bake at 400°F. for 20 minutes or until hot and bubbly.

Zesty Slow-Cooker Italian Pot Roast

MAKES: **4 TO 6 SERVINGS**

Campbell's Kitchen Tip:
For thicker gravy, mix
¼ **cup** all-purpose flour
and ½ **cup** water.
Remove roast from the
cooker. Stir flour mixture
into cooker. Turn heat to
HIGH. Cover and cook
for 10 minutes or until
mixture boils and
thickens.

2½-pound boneless beef bottom round **or** chuck pot roast

½ teaspoon ground black pepper

4 medium potatoes (about 1 pound), cut into quarters

2 cups fresh **or** frozen whole baby carrots

1 stalk celery, cut into 1-inch pieces

1 medium Italian plum tomato, diced

1 can (10¾ ounces) Campbell's® Condensed Tomato Soup

½ cup water

1 tablespoon chopped roasted garlic* **or** fresh garlic

1 teaspoon **each** dried basil leaves, dried oregano leaves **and** dried parsley flakes, crushed

1 teaspoon vinegar

1. Season the roast with the black pepper.

2. Put the potatoes, carrots, celery and tomato in 3½-quart slow cooker. Top with the roast.

3. Stir the soup, water, garlic, basil, oregano, parsley flakes and vinegar in a medium bowl. Pour the soup mixture over the roast and vegetables.

4. Cover and cook on LOW for 10 to 12 hours** or until meat is fork-tender.

5. Remove the roast from the cooker to a cutting board and let it stand for 10 minutes. Thinly slice the roast and arrange on a serving platter. Remove the vegetables with a slotted spoon and put on platter. Pour the juices from the cooker into a gravy boat and serve with the roast and vegetables.

To roast garlic, place whole garlic bulb on piece of aluminum foil. Drizzle with vegetable oil and wrap. Roast at 350°F. for 45 minutes or until soft. Peel and chop garlic.

**Or on HIGH 5 to 6 hours*

Tangy Grilled Beef

MAKES: **6 SERVINGS**

START TO FINISH:
20 minutes

Prep: *5 minutes*
Grill/Cook: *15 minutes*

- 1 can (10¾ ounces) Campbell's® Condensed Tomato Soup
- 2 tablespoons packed brown sugar
- 2 tablespoons lemon juice
- 2 tablespoons vegetable oil
- 1 tablespoon Worcestershire sauce
- 1 teaspoon garlic powder
- ¼ teaspoon dried thyme leaves, crushed
- 1½ pounds boneless beef sirloin steak, ¾-inch thick

1. Stir the soup, sugar, lemon juice, oil, Worcestershire, garlic powder and thyme in a medium bowl.

2. Lightly oil the grill rack and heat the grill to medium. Grill the steak for 10 minutes for medium-rare* or until desired doneness, turning the steak over halfway through cooking and brushing it often with some of the soup mixture.

3. Pour the remaining soup mixture into a 1-quart saucepan. Heat over medium-high heat to a boil. Serve the sauce with the steak.

*The internal temperature of the steak should reach 145°F.

Comfort of
BEEF

Beefy Macaroni Skillet

MAKES: **4 SERVINGS**

START TO FINISH:
15 minutes

Prep: *5 minutes*
Cook: *10 minutes*

- 1   pound ground beef
- 1   medium onion, chopped (about ½ cup)
- 1   can (10¾ ounces) Campbell's® Condensed Tomato Soup
- ¼ cup water
- 1   tablespoon Worcestershire sauce
- ½ cup shredded Cheddar cheese
- 1½ cups cooked corkscrew-shaped **or** elbow macaroni, cooked and drained

1. Cook the beef and onion in a 10-inch skillet over medium-high until the beef is well browned, stirring frequently to break up meat. Pour off any fat.

2. Stir the soup, water, Worcestershire, cheese and pasta into the skillet. Cook and stir until the mixture is hot and bubbling.

Easy Beef Pot Pie

MAKES: **4 SERVINGS**

- ½ of a 15 ounce package refrigerated pie crusts (1 crust)
- 2 cups diced cooked potatoes
- 1 package (10 ounces) frozen mixed vegetables, thawed (about 2 cups)
- 1½ cups diced cooked beef
- 1 can (10¾ ounces) Campbell's® Condensed Golden Mushroom Soup
- ⅓ cup water
- 1 teaspoon Worcestershire sauce
- 1 teaspoon dried thyme leaves, crushed

1. Heat the oven to 400°F. Let the pie crust stand at room temperature for 15 minutes or until it's easy to handle.

2. Put the potatoes, vegetables and beef in a 9-inch deep-dish pie plate or 1½-quart baking dish.

3. Stir the soup, water, Worcestershire and thyme in a small bowl. Pour the soup mixture over the beef mixture. Gently put the pie crust over the beef mixture. Crimp or roll the edges to seal it to the dish. Cut slits in the crust with a knife.

4. Bake for 35 minutes or until hot and the crust is golden brown.

START TO FINISH:
55 minutes

Prep: *20 minutes*
Bake: *35 minutes*

Time-Saving Tip:
To thaw the vegetables, microwave on HIGH for 2 minutes.

Comfort of BEEF

Japanese Beef Stir-Fry

MAKES: **8 SERVINGS**

Make Ahead Tip:
Prepare the vegetables and place in resealable plastic bags. Refrigerate overnight.

3 tablespoons cornstarch
1 can (10½ ounces) Campbell's® Condensed Beef Broth
½ cup soy sauce
2 tablespoons sugar
2 tablespoons vegetable oil
2 pounds boneless beef sirloin **or** top round steak, ¾-inch thick, cut in thin strips
4 cups sliced shiitake mushrooms (about 7 ounces)
1 head Chinese cabbage (bok choy), thinly sliced (about 6 cups)
2 medium red peppers, cut into 2-inch-long strips (about 3 cups)
3 stalks celery, sliced (about 1½ cups)
2 medium green onions, cut into 2-inch pieces (about ½ cup)
Hot cooked rice

1. Stir the cornstarch, broth, soy and sugar in a small cup. Set the mixture aside.

2. Heat **1 tablespoon** of the oil in 4-quart saucepan or wok over high heat. Add the beef in 2 batches and stir-fry until it's browned. Remove the beef with a slotted spoon and set it aside.

3. Reduce the heat to medium and add the remaining oil. Add the mushrooms, cabbage, peppers, celery and green onions in 2 batches. Stir-fry until the vegetables are tender-crisp. Remove the vegetables with a slotted spoon and set them aside.

4. Stir the cornstarch mixture and stir it into the saucepan. Cook and stir until the mixture boils and thickens. Return the beef and vegetables to the saucepan and cook until the mixture is hot and bubbling. Serve over rice.

Savory Pot Roast

MAKES: **8 SERVINGS**

START TO FINISH:
3 hours, 5 minutes

Prep: *15 minutes*

Cook: *2 hours,*
50 minutes

2   tablespoons vegetable oil

    3½- to 4-pound boneless beef bottom round **or** chuck pot roast

1   can (10¾ ounces) Campbell's® Condensed Cream of Mushroom Soup (Regular **or** 98% Fat Free)

1¼ cups water

1   pouch Campbell's® Dry Onion Soup & Recipe Mix

6   medium potatoes, cut into quarters

6   medium carrots, cut into 2-inch pieces

2   tablespoons all-purpose flour

1. Heat the oil in a 4-quart saucepan over medium-high heat. Add the roast and cook until it's well browned on all sides. Pour off any fat.

2. Add the mushroom soup, **1 cup** water and onion soup mix. Heat to a boil. Reduce the heat to low. Cover and cook for 1 hour, 30 minutes.

3. Add the potatoes and carrots. Cover and cook for 1 hour more or until the meat and vegetables are fork-tender. Remove the roast and vegetables to serving platter.

4. Stir the flour and remaining water in a small cup and stir into the soup mixture. Cook and stir over medium-high heat until the mixture boils and thickens. Serve with the roast and vegetables.

Comfort of
BEEF

Mexican Lasagna

MAKES: **8 SERVINGS**

START TO FINISH:
55 minutes

Prep: *30 minutes*

Bake: *20 minutes*

Stand: *5 minutes*

Easy Substitution Tip:
Substitute **1 pound** skinless, boneless chicken breast halves, cut into cubes, for the ground beef.

   1   pound ground beef
   1   large green pepper, chopped (about 1 cup)
   2   cups Prego® Traditional Italian Sauce
1½   cups Pace® Picante Sauce
   1   tablespoon chili powder
   8   flour tortillas (6-inch)
   2   cups shredded Cheddar cheese (8 ounces)
   2   cans (2¼ ounces **each**) sliced pitted ripe
         olives, drained

1. Cook the beef and pepper in a 10-inch skillet over medium-high heat until the beef is well browned, stirring frequently to break up meat. Pour off any fat.

2. Stir the Italian sauce, **1 cup** picante sauce and chili powder into the skillet. Heat to a boil. Reduce the heat to low. Cook for 10 minutes.

3. Spread the remaining picante sauce in a 13×9×2-inch shallow baking dish. Arrange **4** tortillas in the dish. Top with **half** of the beef mixture, **1 cup** of the cheese and **half** of the olives. Repeat the layers.

4. Bake at 350°F. for 20 minutes or until hot. Let the lasagna stand for 5 minutes before serving.

Shortcut Beef Stew

MAKES: **4 SERVINGS**

- 1 tablespoon vegetable oil
- 1 pound boneless beef sirloin steak, ¾-inch thick, cut into 1-inch pieces
- 1 can (10¾ ounces) Campbell's® Condensed Tomato Soup
- 1 can (10½ ounces) Campbell's® Condensed French Onion Soup
- 1 tablespoon Worcestershire sauce
- 1 bag (24 ounces) frozen vegetables for stew (potatoes, carrots, celery)

1. Heat the oil in a 10-inch skillet over medium-high heat. Add the beef and cook until it's well browned, stirring often.

2. Stir the soups, Worcestershire and vegetables into the skillet. Heat to a boil. Reduce the heat to low. Cover and cook for 10 minutes or until the vegetables are tender.

START TO FINISH:
25 minutes

Prep: *5 minutes*
Cook: *20 minutes*

Easy Substitution Tip:
Substitute 5 **cups** frozen vegetables (carrots, small whole onions, cut green beans, cauliflower, zucchini, peas or lima beans) for the frozen vegetables for stew.

Steak & Mushroom Florentine

START TO FINISH:
20 minutes

Prep/Cook: *20 minutes*

MAKES: **4 SERVINGS**

- 2 tablespoons vegetable oil
- 1 pound boneless beef sirloin **or** top round steak, ¾-inch thick, cut into thin strips
- 1 small onion, sliced (about ¼ cup)
- 4 cups baby spinach leaves, washed
- 1 can (10¾ ounces) Campbell's® Condensed Cream of Mushroom Soup (Regular **or** 98% Fat Free)
- 1 cup water
- 1 large tomato, thickly sliced
  Freshly ground black pepper

1. Heat **1 tablespoon** of the oil in 10-inch medium nonstick skillet over medium-high heat. Add the beef and cook and stir until it's well browned. Remove the beef with a slotted spoon and set it aside.

2. Reduce the heat to medium and add the remaining oil. Add the onion. Cook and stir until onion is tender-crisp. Add the spinach and cook just until the spinach wilts.

3. Stir the soup and water into the skillet. Heat to a boil. Return the beef to the skillet and cook until the mixture is hot and bubbling. Serve over the tomato. Season to taste with black pepper.

Souper Sloppy Joes

MAKES: **6 SANDWICHES**

START TO FINISH:
15 minutes

Prep/Cook: *15 minutes*

1 **pound ground beef**
1 **can (10¾ ounces) Campbell's® Condensed Tomato Soup**
¼ **cup water**
1 **tablespoon prepared yellow mustard**
6 **hamburger rolls, split**

1. Cook the beef in a 10-inch skillet over medium-high heat until the beef is well browned, stirring frequently to break up meat. Pour off any fat.

2. Stir the soup, water and mustard into the skillet. Cook and stir until the mixture is hot and bubbling.

3. Divide the beef mixture among the rolls.

Slow Cooker Hearty Beef & Bean Chili

START TO FINISH:
*8 to 10 hours,
15 minutes*

Prep: *15 minutes*

Cook: *8 to 10 hours*

MAKES: **6 SERVINGS**

1½ pounds ground beef
 1 can (10¾ ounces) Campbell's® Condensed
    Tomato Soup
½ cup water
¼ cup chili powder
 2 teaspoons ground cumin
 2 cloves garlic, minced
 1 large onion, chopped (about 1 cup)
 2 cans (about 15 ounces **each**) red kidney
    beans, drained
 1 can (14½ ounces) diced tomatoes

1. Cook the beef in a 10-inch skillet over medium-high heat until the beef is well browned, stirring frequently to break up meat. Remove the beef with a slotted spoon and put in a 3½-quart slow cooker.

2. Stir the soup, water, chili powder, cumin, garlic, onion, beans and tomatoes into the cooker.

3. Cover and cook on LOW for 8 to 10 hours*.

*Or on HIGH for 4 to 5 hours

Weekday Pot Roast & Vegetables

MAKES: **6 TO 8 SERVINGS**

START TO FINISH:
10 to 12 hours,
25 minutes

Prep: *15 minutes*

Cook: *10 to 12 hours*

Stand: *10 minutes*

2- to 2½-pound boneless beef bottom round
  or chuck pot roast
1 teaspoon garlic powder
1 tablespoon vegetable oil
4 medium potatoes (about 1 pound), each cut
  into 6 wedges
3 cups fresh **or** frozen baby carrots
1 medium onion, thickly sliced (about ¾ cup)
2 teaspoons dried basil leaves, crushed
2 cans (10¼ ounces **each**) Campbell's® Beef
  Gravy

1. Season roast with the garlic powder. Heat the oil in a 10-inch skillet over medium-high heat. Add the roast and cook until it's browned on all sides.

2. Stir the potatoes, carrots, onion and basil in a 3½-quart slow cooker. Top with the roast. Pour the gravy over the roast and vegetables.

3. Cover and cook on LOW for 10 to 12 hours* or until the meat is fork-tender.

4. Remove the roast from the cooker to a cutting board and let it stand for 10 minutes. Thinly slice the roast and arrange on a serving platter. Remove the vegetables with a slotted spoon and put on platter. Pour the juices from the cooker into a gravy boat and serve with the roast and vegetables.

*Or on HIGH for 5 to 6 hours

Cheeseburger Chowder

MAKES: **8 SERVINGS**

START TO FINISH:
30 minutes

Prep: *10 minutes*
Cook: *20 minutes*

- 1 pound ground beef
- 1 large onion, chopped (about 1 cup)
- 2 cans (26 ounces **each**) Campbell's® Condensed Cream of Mushroom Soup (Regular **or** 98% Fat Free)
- 2 soup cans milk
- 1 cup finely shredded Cheddar cheese (4 ounces)
- 1 cup Pepperidge Farm® Generous Cut Seasoned Croutons

1. Cook the beef and onion in a 3-quart saucepan over medium-high heat until the beef is well browned, stirring frequently to break up meat. Pour off any fat.

2. Stir the soup and milk into the saucepan. Cook until the mixture is hot and bubbling. Stir in ½ **cup** of the cheese. Cook and stir until the cheese melts.

3. Divide the soup among **8** serving bowls. Top each bowl of soup with **1 tablespoon** of the remaining cheese and **2 tablespoons** croutons.

Smokin' Texas Chili

MAKES: **6 SERVINGS**

START TO FINISH:
2 hours

Prep: *15 minutes*

Cook: *1 hour,*
45 minutes

2 tablespoons olive oil

1½ pounds boneless beef sirloin **or** top round
steak, ¾-inch thick, cut into ½-inch pieces

1 medium onion, chopped (about ½ cup)

2 cloves garlic, minced

3 cups Pace® Chunky Salsa, any variety

½ cup water

1 tablespoon chili powder

1 teaspoon ground cumin

1 can (about 15 ounces) red kidney beans,
rinsed and drained

¼ cup chopped fresh cilantro leaves

Chili Toppings: chopped tomatoes, chopped
onions or shredded cheese (optional)

1. Heat **1 tablespoon** oil in a 4-quart saucepan
over medium-high heat. Add the beef in 2 batches
and cook until it's well browned on all sides, stirring
often. Remove the beef with a slotted spoon and
set it aside.

2. Reduce the heat to medium and add the
remaining oil. Add the onion. Cook and stir until
the onion is tender. Add the garlic and cook for
30 seconds.

3. Stir the salsa, water, chili powder, cumin and
beans into the saucepan. Heat to a boil. Return the
beef to the saucepan. Reduce the heat to low.
Cover and cook for 1 hour. Uncover and cook for
30 minutes more or until the meat is fork-tender.
Sprinkle with cilantro and serve with *Chili Toppings*,
if desired.

Inviting

PORK

Sausage, Beef & Bean Casserole

MAKES: **6 SERVINGS**

- 1 pound sweet Italian pork sausage, cut into 1-inch pieces
- ½ pound ground beef
- 1 small onion, chopped (about ¼ cup)
- 1 bag (6 ounces) baby spinach leaves, washed
- 1 can (10¾ ounces) Campbell's® Condensed Cream of Mushroom Soup (Regular **or** 98% Fat Free)
- ¼ cup milk
- 1 can (about 15 ounces) white kidney (cannellini) beans, rinsed and drained
- 1 cup Pepperidge Farm® Herb Seasoned Stuffing
- ½ cup crumbled blue cheese **or** shredded Cheddar cheese

1. Cook the sausage, beef and onion in a 12-inch nonstick skillet or 5-quart saucepot until the meats are well browned, stirring frequently to break up meat. Pour off fat. Add the spinach and cook until the spinach wilts.

2. Stir the soup, milk and beans into the skillet. Spoon the mixture into a 2-quart casserole.

3. Stir the stuffing and cheese in a small bowl. Sprinkle around the edge of the dish.

4. Bake at 350°F. for 30 minutes or until hot and bubbly and the internal temperature of the sausage mixture is 160°F.

BBQ Pork Chops

MAKES: **6 SERVINGS**

START TO FINISH:
1 hour, 20 minutes

Prep: *20 minutes*

Bake: *1 hour*

6 boneless pork chops, ¾-inch thick (about 1½ pounds)
  Ground black pepper
1 tablespoon vegetable oil
1 can (10¾ ounces) Campbell's® Condensed Tomato Soup
½ cup water
2 tablespoons cider vinegar
2 tablespoons molasses
1 tablespoon Worcestershire sauce
1 teaspoon minced garlic
½ teaspoon dried thyme leaves, crushed
1 bag (16 ounces) baby carrots (about 2½ cups)
1 medium onion, sliced (about ½ cup)
  Hot cooked cholesterol-free medium noodle-style pasta

1. Season the pork chops with black pepper. Heat the oil in an oven-safe 12-inch skillet over medium-high heat. Add the pork chops and cook until the chops are well browned on both sides. Remove the chops and set them aside.

2. Stir the soup, water, vinegar, molasses, Worcestershire, garlic, thyme, carrots and onion into the skillet. Heat to a boil. Return the chops to the skillet. Cover and bake at 350°F. for 1 hour or until the chops are cooked through but slightly pink in center*. Serve with the pasta.

*The internal temperature of the pork should reach 160°F.

Cranberry Dijon Pork Chops

MAKES: **4 SERVINGS**

- 1 tablespoon olive oil
- 4 boneless pork chops, 1-inch thick (about 1¼ pounds)
- 1 can (10¾ ounces) Campbell's® Condensed Cream of Celery Soup (Regular **or** 98% Fat Free)
- ½ cup cranberry juice
- 2 tablespoons Dijon-style mustard
- ¼ teaspoon dried thyme leaves, crushed
- ¼ cup dried cranberries **or** cherries
  Hot cooked noodles

1. Heat the oil in a 10-inch oven-safe skillet over medium-high heat. Add the pork chops and cook until the chops are well browned on both sides. Remove the pork chops and set them aside.

2. Stir the soup, cranberry juice, mustard and thyme into the skillet. Heat to a boil. Return the pork chops to the skillet and cover.

3. Bake at 350°F. for 45 minutes or until chops are cooked through but slightly pink in center*. Place the pork chops on a serving plate. Stir the cranberries into the skillet. Serve the sauce with the pork and noodles.

*The internal temperature of the pork should reach 160°F.

Cassoulet

MAKES: **8 SERVINGS**

Time-Saving Tip:
To save prep time, ask your butcher to cut the lamb and pork into 1-inch pieces.

Make Ahead Tip:
Cassoulet is best when prepared and fully cooked the day ahead. Refrigerate. To reheat, bake at 300°F. for 1 hour or until hot. Add additional Swanson® Beef Broth to keep beans from drying out.

4	slices thick-cut bacon (about 4 ounces), diced
1	pound **each** boneless leg of lamb **and** boneless pork loin, cut into 1-inch pieces
½	pound kielbasa, sliced diagonally
¼	cup chopped fresh parsley
3	cloves garlic, minced
2	tablespoons grated lemon peel (about 1 lemon)
1	teaspoon dried thyme leaves, crushed
2	cans (15 ounces **each**) great Northern beans, rinsed and drained
2	bay leaves
1	can (14½ ounces) Campbell's® Beef Gravy
1	cup Swanson® Beef Broth (Regular, Lower Sodium **or** Certified Organic)
2	tablespoons tomato paste
½	cup dry bread crumbs

1. Cook bacon in a 6-quart oven-safe saucepot over medium-high heat for 5 minutes or until the bacon is crisp. Remove the bacon with a slotted spoon and drain on paper towels.

2. Add the lamb, pork and kielbasa in 2 batches and cook in the hot drippings until well browned. Remove with a slotted spoon and set the lamb, pork and kielbasa aside.

3. Stir the parsley, garlic, lemon peel and thyme in a small cup.

4. Layer **1 cup** of the beans, **half** of **each** of the bacon, lamb, pork, sausage, parsley mixture and 1 bay leaf in the saucepot. Repeat layers, using **half** the remaining beans. Top with remaining beans.

5. Stir the gravy, broth and tomato paste in a small bowl. Pour the gravy mixture over meat and beans.

6. Bake at 350°F. for 1 hour. Sprinkle with bread crumbs. Bake for 1 hour more or until lamb is fork-tender. Discard the bay leaves. Serve immediately or cool 2 hours, cover and refrigerate at least 8 hours or overnight.

Beer & Kraut Brats

MAKES: **4 SERVINGS**

START TO FINISH:
35 minutes

Prep: *10 minutes*
Cook: *25 minutes*

½ pound thick-cut bacon, diced
1 pound bratwurst, cut into 2-inch pieces
1 can (12 fluid ounces) beer
1 can (10½ ounces) Campbell's® Condensed French Onion Soup
¼ cup packed brown sugar
1 package (16 ounces) fresh sauerkraut, drained (about 3 cups)
Hot mashed potatoes **or** egg noodles

1. Cook bacon in a 12-inch skillet over medium-high heat for 5 minutes or until the bacon is crisp. Remove the bacon with a slotted spoon and drain on paper towels. Pour off drippings.

2. Add the bratwurst and cook until it's well browned.

3. Stir the beer, soup, brown sugar, sauerkraut and bacon into the skillet. Heat to a boil. Reduce the heat to low.

4. Cook for 15 minutes or until the bratwurst reaches an internal temperature of 160°F., stirring the mixture a few times while it's cooking. Serve over potatoes or noodles.

Cavatelli with Sausage & Broccoli

MAKES: **6 SERVINGS**

START TO FINISH:
40 minutes

Prep: *10 minutes*
Cook: *30 minutes*

  1   package (16 ounces) frozen cavatelli pasta
  1   tablespoon olive oil
  1   pound sweet Italian pork sausage, casing removed
  1   tablespoon butter
  2   cloves garlic, minced
  1   bag (about 16 ounces) frozen broccoli flowerets
1¾   cups Swanson® Chicken Broth (Regular, Natural Goodness™ **or** Certified Organic)
  2   tablespoons grated Romano cheese
      Crushed red pepper

1. Prepare the pasta according to the package directions. Drain the pasta well in a colander. Return pasta to the saucepot.

2. Heat the oil in a 10-inch skillet over medium-high heat. Add the sausage and cook until it's well browned, stirring frequently to break up meat. Remove the sausage with a slotted spoon and set it aside.

3. Reduce the heat to medium and add the butter to the skillet. Add the garlic and cook for about 2 minutes or until golden.

4. Add the broccoli. Cook and stir for 5 minutes until the broccoli is tender-crisp.

5. Stir the broth into the skillet. Heat to a boil. Remove from the heat.

6. Add the broccoli mixture, sausage and cheese to saucepot. Cook and stir over medium heat for 10 minutes or until the sausage reaches an internal temperature of 160°F. and the sauce thickens. Serve with red pepper and additional cheese, if desired.

Creamy Pork Sauté

MAKES: **4 SERVINGS**

START TO FINISH:
25 minutes

Prep: *10 minutes*
Cook: *15 minutes*

2 tablespoons vegetable oil

1 pound boneless pork loin, cut into thin strips

2 stalks celery, sliced (about 1 cup)

1 medium onion, chopped (about ½ cup)

½ teaspoon dried thyme leaves, crushed

1 can (10¾ ounces) Campbell's® Condensed Cream of Celery Soup (Regular **or** 98% Fat Free)

¼ cup water

Hot cooked rice

1. Heat **1 tablespoon** of the oil in a 10-inch skillet over medium-high heat. Add the pork and cook until it's well browned, stirring often. Remove the pork with a slotted spoon and set it aside.

2. Reduce the heat to medium and add the remaining oil. Add the celery, onion and thyme. Cook and stir until the vegetables are tender.

3. Stir the soup and water into the skillet. Heat to a boil. Return the pork to the skillet and cook until hot and bubbling. Serve over the rice.

Picante Pork Stew

MAKES: **4 SERVINGS**

START TO FINISH:
45 minutes

Prep: *20 minutes*
Cook: *25 minutes*

   3 tablespoons cornstarch
1¾ cups Swanson® Vegetable Broth (Regular **or** Certified Organic)
   2 tablespoons vegetable oil
   1 pound boneless pork loin, cut into thin strips
   4 cups cut-up fresh vegetables*
   ½ cup Pace® Picante Sauce

1. Stir the cornstarch and broth in a small bowl. Set the mixture aside.

2. Heat **1 tablespoon** of the oil in a 4-quart saucepan over medium-high heat. Add the pork and cook until well browned, stirring often. Remove the pork with a slotted spoon and set it aside.

3. Reduce the heat to medium and add the remaining oil. Add the vegetables and cook until the vegetables are tender-crisp. Pour off any fat.

4. Stir the picante sauce into the saucepan. Stir cornstarch mixture and stir it into the saucepan. Cook and stir until mixture boils and thickens. Return the pork to the pan. Cook until hot and bubbling.

Use asparagus cut into 2-inch pieces, red pepper cut into 2-inch-long strips and sliced onions.

Hearty Sausage & Rice Casserole

MAKES: **6 SERVINGS**

Easy Substitution Tip:
For an extra-special touch, substitute 1 package (8 ounces) baby portobello mushrooms, sliced, for the sliced mushrooms.

- 1 pound bulk pork sausage
- 1 package (8 ounces) sliced mushrooms (about 3 cups)
- 2 large stalks celery, coarsely chopped (about 1 cup)
- 1 large red pepper, coarsely chopped (about 1 cup)
- 1 large onion, coarsely chopped (about 1 cup)
- 1 teaspoon dried thyme leaves, crushed
- ½ teaspoon dried marjoram leaves, crushed
- 1¾ cups Swanson® Chicken Broth (Regular, Natural Goodness™ **or** Certified Organic)
- 1 can (10¾ ounces) Campbell's® Condensed Cream of Mushroom Soup (Regular **or** 98% Fat Free)
- 1 box (6 ounces) long-grain white and wild rice mix
- 1 cup shredded Cheddar cheese (4 ounces)

1. Cook the sausage in a 12-inch skillet over medium-high heat until it's well browned, stirring frequently to break up meat. Remove the sausage with a slotted spoon and set it aside. Pour off any fat.

2. Reduce the heat to medium. Add the mushrooms, celery, pepper, onion, thyme, marjoram and seasoning packet from the rice mix. Cook and stir until the vegetables are tender-crisp.

3. Stir the broth, soup, rice mix and ½ **cup** of the cheese in a 13×9×2-inch shallow baking dish. Stir in the sausage and the vegetable mixture. Cover the dish with foil.

4. Bake at 375°F. for 1 hour or until the casserole is hot and bubbly and the rice is tender. Stir the rice mixture before serving. Sprinkle with the remaining cheese.

Hearty Mixed Bean Stew with Sausage

START TO FINISH:
*8 to 9 hours,
15 minutes*

Prep: *15 minutes*

Cook: *8 to 9 hours*

MAKES: **8 SERVINGS**

¾ pound sweet Italian pork sausage, casing removed

10 cups Swanson® Chicken Broth (Regular, Natural Goodness™ **or** Certified Organic)

¼ teaspoon ground black pepper

2 medium carrots, chopped (about ⅔ cup)

1 stalk celery, chopped (about ½ cup)

4 ounces **each** dried pinto, navy **and** kidney beans (about ¾ cup **each**)

6 sun-dried tomatoes in oil, drained and thinly sliced (about ¼ cup)

Grated Parmesan cheese

1. Cook the sausage in a 10-inch skillet over medium-high heat until it's well browned, stirring frequently to break up meat. Remove the sausage with a slotted spoon and put in a 5- to 5½-quart slow cooker.

2. Stir in the broth, black pepper, carrots, celery and pinto, navy and kidney beans.

3. Cover and cook on LOW for 7 or 8 hours*.

4. Stir in tomatoes. Cover and cook for 1 hour more or until the beans are tender. Serve with cheese.

*Or on HIGH for 4 to 4¹/₂ hours

Sausage-Stuffed Green Peppers

MAKES: **8 SERVINGS**

START TO FINISH:
1 hour

Prep: *20 minutes*
Bake: *40 minutes*

- 4 **medium green peppers**
- 1 **tablespoon vegetable oil**
- 1 **pound sweet Italian pork sausage, casing removed**
- 1 **medium onion, chopped (about ½ cup)**
- 1 **teaspoon dried oregano leaves, crushed**
- 1 **cup shredded part-skim mozzarella cheese (4 ounces)**
- 2 **cups Prego® Traditional Italian Sauce**

1. Cut a thin slice from the top of each pepper, cut in half lengthwise and discard the seeds and white membranes. Place the pepper shells in a 13×9×2-inch shallow baking dish or roasting pan and set them aside.

2. Heat the oil in a 10-inch skillet over medium-high heat. Add the sausage and cook until it's well browned, stirring frequently to break up meat. Add the onion and oregano. Cook and stir until the onion is tender. Pour off any fat. Stir in the cheese.

3. Spoon the sausage mixture into the pepper shells. Pour the Italian sauce over the peppers. Cover the dish with foil.

4. Bake at 400°F. for 40 minutes or until sausage reaches an internal temperature of 160°F. and the peppers are tender.

Roast Pork with Green Apples & Golden Squash

MAKES: **8 SERVINGS**

Vegetable cooking spray

2 (¾ pound **each**) whole pork tenderloins

1 teaspoon olive oil

¼ teaspoon coarsely ground black pepper

3 large Granny Smith apples, cored and thickly sliced

1 butternut squash (about 1½ pounds), peeled, seeded and cubed (about 4 cups)

2 tablespoons packed brown sugar

½ teaspoon ground cinnamon

1¾ cups Swanson® Chicken Broth (Regular, Natural Goodness™ **or** Certified Organic)

2 teaspoons all-purpose flour

1. Heat the oven to 425°F. Spray a 17×11-inch roasting pan with cooking spray.

2. Brush the pork with the oil and sprinkle with the black pepper. Put the pork in the prepared pan.

3. Put the apples, squash, brown sugar, cinnamon and ½ **cup** broth in a large bowl. Toss to coat with the broth mixture. Add the squash mixture to the pan.

4. Bake for 25 minutes or until the pork is cooked through but slightly pink in center*, stirring the squash mixture once while it's cooking. Remove the pork from the pan to a cutting board and let it stand for 10 minutes. Continue to bake the squash mixture for 15 minutes more or until browned. Remove the squash mixture from the pan with a slotted spoon.

5. Stir the flour into the drippings in the roasting pan. Cook and stir over medium heat for 1 minute then gradually stir in the remaining broth. Cook and stir until the mixture boils and thickens. Thinly slice the pork and arrange on a serving platter with the vegetables. Pour the sauce into a gravy boat and serve with the pork.

*The internal temperature of the pork should reach 155°F. During the standing time, the temperature will continue to increase to 160°F.

Inviting
PORK

Unstuffed Pork Chops

MAKES: **6 SERVINGS**

- 6 bone-in loin pork chops (¾-inch thick)
- ¼ teaspoon ground black pepper
- 1 tablespoon vegetable oil
- 1 can (10½ ounces) Campbell's® Condensed Chicken Broth
- 4 tablespoons butter
- 2 stalks celery, chopped (about 1 cup)
- 1 medium onion, chopped (about ½ cup)
- 4 cups Pepperidge Farm® Herbed Seasoned Stuffing

1. Season the pork chops with black pepper. Heat the oil in a 12-inch skillet over medium-high heat. Add the pork chops and cook until the chops are well browned on both sides.

2. Heat the broth and butter in a 3-quart saucepan over medium-high heat to a boil. Add the celery and onion and cook for 2 minutes or until the vegetables are tender. Add the stuffing and stir lightly to coat. Spoon the stuffing mixture into a 13×9×2-inch shallow baking dish. Top with the pork chops.

3. Bake at 400°F. for 20 minutes or until the chops are cooked through but slightly pink in center* and the stuffing reaches 165°F.

The internal temperature of the pork should reach 160°F.

Sausage & Pepper Heros

MAKES: **12 SERVINGS**

- 3 pounds sweet **or** hot Italian pork sausage, cut into 2-inch pieces
- 1 jar (67 ounces) Prego® Traditional Italian Sauce (7½ cups)
- 3 medium green peppers, cut into 2-inch-long strips (about 4½ cups)
- 3 medium onions, sliced (about 1½ cups)
- 12 long sandwich rolls (7 inches), split
  Grated Parmesan cheese

1. Put the sausage in a 16½×12×2½-inch disposable foil pan.

2. Bake at 425°F. for 45 minutes or until the sausage is browned. Carefully pour off juices that are in the pan.

3. Stir in the Italian sauce, peppers and onions. Cover the pan with foil.

4. Bake for 45 minutes more or until the sausage reaches an internal temperature of 160°F.

5. Divide the sausage and peppers among the roll halves. Top with the cheese and remaining roll halves.

Pennsylvania Dutch Ham & Noodle Casserole

MAKES: **4 SERVINGS**

Easy Substitution Tip:
Substitute cooked chicken or turkey for ham.

1 tablespoon vegetable oil

2 cups cubed cooked ham (about 1 pound)

1 medium onion, chopped (about ½ cup)

1 can (10¾ ounces) Campbell's® Condensed Cream of Mushroom Soup (Regular **or** 98% Fat Free)

8 ounces extra-sharp Cheddar cheese, sliced

8 ounces extra-wide egg noodles (2 cups), cooked and drained

1. Heat the oil in a 4-quart saucepan over medium-high heat. Add the ham and onion. Cook and stir until the onion is tender.

2. Stir the soup into the saucepan. Reduce the heat to medium. Cook and stir for 5 minutes. Add the cheese and stir until the cheese melts. Gently stir in the noodles. Heat through, stirring often.

Pork & Corn Stuffing Bake

MAKES: **4 SERVINGS**

START TO FINISH:
40 minutes

Prep: *10 minutes*
Bake: *30 minutes*

Vegetable cooking spray

1 can (10¾ ounces) Campbell's® Condensed Cream of Celery Soup (Regular **or** 98% Fat Free)

½ cup whole kernel corn

1 small onion, finely chopped (about ¼ cup)

¼ cup finely chopped celery

1½ cups Pepperidge Farm® Cornbread Stuffing **or** Herb Seasoned Stuffing

4 boneless pork chops, ¾-inch thick (about 1 pound)

1 tablespoon packed brown sugar

1 teaspoon spicy-brown mustard

1. Spray a 9-inch pie plate with the cooking spray. Stir the soup, corn, onion, celery and stuffing in the prepared dish. Top with the chops.

2. Stir the brown sugar and mustard in a small cup. Spoon over the chops.

3. Bake at 400°F. for 30 minutes or until the chops are cooked through but slightly pink in center*.

*The internal temperature of the pork should reach 160°F.

Gumbo Casserole

MAKES: **4 SERVINGS**

2 cans (10¾ ounces **each**) Campbell's®
    Condensed Chicken Gumbo Soup
1 soup can water
1 teaspoon dried minced onion
½ teaspoon Cajun seasoning
½ teaspoon garlic powder
1 cup frozen okra, thawed
¾ cup **uncooked** instant white rice
½ pound cooked ham, diced (about 1½ cups)
½ pound cooked shrimp, peeled and deveined

1. Stir the soup, water, onion, Cajun seasoning, garlic powder, okra, rice, ham and shrimp in a 2-quart casserole.

2. Bake at 375°F. for 35 minutes or until hot. Stir before serving. Serve in bowls.

Saucy Creole Pork Chops

MAKES: **4 SERVINGS**

START TO FINISH:
30 minutes

Prep: *5 minutes*
Cook: *25 minutes*

4 boneless pork chops, ¾-inch thick (about 1 pound)

1½ teaspoons Creole **or** Cajun seasoning

2 tablespoons vegetable **or** canola oil

1 medium onion, chopped (about ½ cup)

2 cloves garlic, minced

1 can (10¾ ounces) Campbell's Condensed Cream of Celery Soup (Regular **or** 98% Fat Free)

⅓ cup water

1 tablespoon chopped fresh parsley

1 can (14½ ounces) diced tomatoes, undrained

Hot cooked rice

1. Season the pork chops with the Creole seasoning.

2. Heat **1 tablespoon** of the oil in a 10-inch skillet over medium-high heat. Add the pork chops and cook until they're well browned on both sides. Remove the chops and set them aside.

3. Reduce the heat to medium and add the remaining oil. Add the onion and garlic. Cook and stir until the onion is tender-crisp. Pour off any fat.

4. Stir the soup, water, parsley and tomatoes into the skillet. Heat to a boil. Return the pork chops to the skillet and cook for 5 minutes or until the chops are slightly pink in the center*. Serve with the rice.

*The internal temperature of the pork should reach 160°F.

Casseroles, One-Dish Meals and More   **61**

Spiral Ham with Mango Salsa

Easy Substitution Tip:
Substitute chopped fresh cilantro leaves for the green onions.

MAKES: 24 SERVINGS

- 1   tablespoon butter
- 1   medium onion, chopped (about ½ cup)
- 1½ cups Swanson® Chicken Broth (Regular, Natural Goodness™ **or** Certified Organic)
- ½   cup mango juice **or** nectar
- 1   package (6 ounces) dried mango, coarsely chopped
- ⅓   cup packed brown sugar
- 2   medium green onions, chopped (about ¼ cup)
- 9-pound fully cooked bone-in **or** 6-pound fully cooked boneless spiral cut ham

1. Heat the butter in a 2-quart saucepan over medium-high heat. Add the onion and cook until it's tender. Stir in the broth, mango juice, dried mango and brown sugar. Heat to a boil. Reduce the heat to low. Cook for 10 minutes or until the mixture thickens. Let cool slightly.

2. Place a strainer over a medium bowl. Pour the broth mixture through the strainer. Reserve the broth mixture to glaze the ham. Put the strained mango mixture in a small bowl. Stir in the green onions. Cover and refrigerate until serving time.

3. Place the ham in a 17×11-inch roasting pan and cover loosely with foil. Bake at 325°F. for 1½ hours. Remove the foil. Spoon the broth mixture over the ham. Bake for 30 minutes more or until the internal temperature of the ham reaches 140°F., basting the ham frequently with the pan drippings. Serve the ham with the mango salsa.

Sausage & Escarole Soup

MAKES: **6 SERVINGS**

START TO FINISH:
2 hours, 45 minutes

Prep: *1 hour*

Cook: *1 hour,*
45 minutes

- 1 cup dried navy beans
- 1 pound sweet Italian pork sausage, casing removed
- 1 large onion, thinly sliced (about 1 cup)
- 2 cloves garlic, thinly sliced
- 6 cups Swanson® Chicken Broth (Regular, Natural Goodness™ **or** Certified Organic)
- 1 head escarole (about 1 pound), chopped (about 8 cups)
- Grated Parmesan cheese
- Freshly ground black pepper

1. Soak the beans according to the package directions. Drain.

2. Cook the sausage in a 4-quart saucepan over medium-high heat until the sausage is well browned, stirring frequently to break up meat. Remove the sausage with a slotted spoon and set it aside.

3. Add the onion and cook for 2 minutes. Add the garlic and cook for 30 seconds.

4. Stir the broth and the drained beans into the saucepan. Heat to a boil. Cover and cook over low heat for 1 hour, 30 minutes or until the beans are tender.

5. Add the escarole. Return the sausage to the pan. Cover and cook for 5 minutes or until the escarole is tender. Serve the soup with the cheese and black pepper.

Hearty Pork Stew

MAKES: **8 SERVINGS**

START TO FINISH:
*7 to 8 hours,
25 minutes*

Prep: *25 minutes*

Cook: *7 to 8 hours*

- 2 pounds sweet potatoes, peeled and cut into 2-inch pieces (about 2 cups)
- 2-pound boneless pork shoulder, cut into 1-inch pieces
- 1 can (14½ ounces) Campbell's® Chicken Gravy
- 1 teaspoon dried thyme leaves, crushed
- ½ teaspoon crushed red pepper
- 1 can (15 ounces) black-eyed peas, rinsed and drained

1. Put the potatoes in a 4- to 6-quart slow cooker. Top with the pork.

2. Stir the gravy, thyme, red pepper and peas in a small bowl. Pour over the pork and potatoes.

3. Cover and cook on LOW for 7 to 8 hours* or until the meat is fork-tender.

Or on HIGH for 4 to 5 hours

Smokin' Baby Back Ribs

MAKES: **8 SERVINGS**

4 pounds baby back pork spareribs

1 tablespoon olive oil

1 large sweet onion, chopped (about 1 cup)

1 can (10¾ ounces) Campbell's® Condensed Tomato Soup

¼ cup packed brown sugar

2 tablespoons cider vinegar

2 to 4 teaspoons hot pepper sauce

1. Line a large shallow roasting pan with foil. Put the ribs in the pan. Cover the pan with foil.

2. Bake at 400°F. for 45 minutes. Uncover the pan and carefully pour off the juices that are in the pan.

3. Heat the oil in a 2-quart saucepan over medium heat. Add the onion and cook until the onion is tender. Add the soup, brown sugar, vinegar and hot pepper sauce and heat to a boil. Reduce the heat to low and cook for 6 minutes or until the sauce slightly thickens.

4. Pour the prepared sauce mixture over the ribs.

5. Bake uncovered for 30 minutes more or until the meat is tender. Cut into serving-size pieces and return to pan. Toss the ribs to coat with the sauce.

START TO FINISH:
1 hour, 25 minutes

Prep: *10 minutes*

Bake: *1 hour, 15 minutes*

Time-Saving Tip:
Prepare the sauce mixture while the ribs are baking.

Pasta with the Works

MAKES: **4 SERVINGS**

START TO FINISH:
25 minutes

Prep: *5 minutes*
Cook: *20 hours*

1 medium green pepper, cut into 2-inch-long
    strips (about 1½ cups)
½ cup thinly sliced pepperoni
2 cups Prego® Italian Sauce with Fresh
    Mushrooms **or** Traditional Italian Sauce
⅓ cup pitted ripe olives, cut in half (optional)
3 cups corkscrew-shaped pasta, cooked and
    drained
1 cup shredded mozzarella cheese (4 ounces)
    Grated Parmesan cheese

1. Cook the pepper and pepperoni in a 10-inch
skillet over medium heat until pepper is tender-
crisp, stirring often.

2. Stir the Italian sauce and olives, if desired, into
the skillet. Heat to a boil. Reduce the heat to low.
Cover and cook for 10 minutes.

3. Stir in the pasta and mozzarella cheese. Serve
with the Parmesan cheese.

Sausage and Bean Ragoût

MAKES: **6 SERVINGS**

START TO FINISH:
35 minutes

Prep: *5 minutes*
Cook: *30 minutes*

2 tablespoons olive oil

1 pound ground beef

1 pound hot Italian pork sausage, casing removed

1 large onion, chopped (1 cup)

4 cloves garlic, minced

3½ cups Swanson® Chicken Broth (Regular, Natural Goodness™ **or** Certified Organic)

¼ cup chopped fresh basil leaves

2 cans (14½ ounces **each**) diced tomatoes seasoned with garlic, oregano & basil

1 can (about 16 ounces) white kidney (cannellini) beans, rinsed and drained

½ cup **uncooked** elbow macaroni

1 bag (6 ounces) baby spinach leaves, washed

⅓ cup grated Romano cheese

1. Heat the oil in a 4-quart saucepan over medium-high heat. Add the beef, sausage and onion and cook until the meats are browned, stirring frequently to break up meat. Add the garlic and cook 30 seconds.

2. Stir the broth, basil, tomatoes and beans into the saucepan. Heat to a boil. Reduce the heat to low. Cover and cook for 10 minutes, stirring occasionally.

3. Stir in the pasta and cook until the pasta is tender but still firm.

4. Stir in the spinach and cook just until spinach wilts, stirring occasionally. Remove from heat and stir in the cheese. Serve with additional cheese.

Tasty
CHICKEN

MEALS FOR EVERY HOUSEHOLD MADE WITH CHICKEN

Chicken in Creamy Sun-Dried Tomato Sauce

MAKES: **8 SERVINGS**

START TO FINISH:
7 to 8 hours,
15 minutes

Prep: *15 minutes*

Cook: *7 to 8 hours*

Easy Substitution Tip:
Substitute Swanson®
Chicken Broth (Regular,
Natural Goodness™ **or**
Certified Organic) for the
wine.

2 cans (10¾ ounces **each**) Campbell's®
   Condensed Cream of Chicken with Herbs
   Soup

1 cup Chablis **or** other dry white wine

¼ cup coarsely chopped pitted kalamata **or**
   oil-cured olives

2 tablespoons drained capers

2 cloves garlic, minced

1 can (14 ounces) artichoke hearts, drained
   and chopped

1 cup drained, coarsely chopped sun-dried
   tomatoes

8 skinless, boneless chicken breast halves

½ cup chopped fresh basil leaves (optional)
   Hot cooked rice, egg noodles **or** seasoned
   mashed potatoes

1. Stir the soup, wine, olives, capers, garlic,
artichokes and tomatoes in a 3½-quart slow cooker.
Add the chicken and turn to coat with the soup
mixture.

2. Cover and cook on LOW for 7 to 8 hours* or
until chicken is cooked through. Sprinkle with basil,
if desired. Serve with rice, noodles or potatoes.

*Or on HIGH for 4 to 5 hours

Chicken Cacciatore

MAKES: **6 SERVINGS**

1¾ cups Swanson® Chicken Broth (Regular,
Natural Goodness™ **or** Certified Organic)

1 teaspoon garlic powder

2 cans (14½ ounces **each**) diced Italian-
style tomatoes

4 cups mushrooms, cut in half (about
12 ounces)

2 large onions, chopped (about 2 cups)

3 pounds chicken parts, skin removed
Hot cooked spaghetti

Campbell's Kitchen Tip:
For thicker sauce,
stir **2 tablespoons**
cornstarch and
2 tablespoons water in a
small cup. Remove the
chicken from cooker.
Stir the cornstarch
mixture into the cooker.
Turn the heat to HIGH.
Cover and cook for
10 minutes or until
mixture boils and
thickens.

1. Stir the broth, garlic powder, tomatoes,
mushrooms and onions in a 3½-quart slow cooker.
Add the chicken and turn to coat with the broth
mixture.

2. Cover and cook on LOW for 7 to 8 hours* or
until the chicken is cooked through. Serve over
the spaghetti.

Or on HIGH for 4 to 5 hours

25-Minute Chicken & Noodles

MAKES: **4 SERVINGS**

START TO FINISH:
25 minutes

Prep: *5 minutes*
Cook: *20 minutes*

1¾ cups Swanson® Chicken Broth (Regular, Natural Goodness™ **or** Certified Organic)

½ teaspoon dried basil leaves, crushed

⅛ teaspoon ground black pepper

2 cups frozen vegetable combination (broccoli, cauliflower, carrots)

2 cups **uncooked** medium egg noodles

2 cups cubed cooked chicken

1. Heat the broth, basil, black pepper and vegetables in a 10-inch skillet over high heat to a boil. Reduce the heat to low. Cover and cook for 5 minutes.

2. Stir the noodles into the skillet. Cover and cook for 5 minutes.

3. Stir in the chicken. Cook until it's hot.

Broccoli Chicken Potato Parmesan

START TO FINISH:
25 minutes

Prep: *5 minutes*
Cook: *20 minutes*

MAKES: **4 SERVINGS**

2 tablespoons vegetable oil

1 pound small red potatoes, sliced ¼-inch thick

1 can (10¾ ounces) Campbell's® Condensed Broccoli Cheese Soup (Regular **or** 98% Fat Free)

½ cup milk

¼ teaspoon garlic powder

2 cups fresh **or** frozen broccoli flowerets

1 package (about 10 ounces) refrigerated cooked chicken breast strips

¼ cup grated Parmesan cheese

1. Heat the oil in a 10-inch skillet over medium heat. Add the potatoes. Cover and cook for 10 minutes, stirring occasionally.

2. Stir the soup, milk, garlic powder, broccoli and chicken into the skillet. Sprinkle with cheese. Heat to a boil. Reduce the heat to low. Cover and cook for 5 minutes or until the potatoes are fork-tender.

2-Step Creamy Chicken & Pasta

MAKES: **4 SERVINGS**

START TO FINISH:
25 minutes

Prep: *5 minutes*

Cook: *20 minutes*

- 1 tablespoon vegetable oil
- 1 pound skinless, boneless chicken breasts, cut into cubes
- 1 can (10¾ ounces) Campbell's® Condensed Cream of Chicken Soup (Regular **or** 98% Fat Free)
- ½ cup water
- 2 boxes (8 ounces **each**) frozen vegetable pasta blend

Easy Substitution Tip:
Substitute Campbell's® Cream of Mushroom **or** Cream of Celery Soup for the Cream of Chicken Soup.

1. Heat the oil in a 10-inch skillet over medium-high heat. Add the chicken and cook until it's well browned, stirring often.

2. Stir the soup, water and pasta blend into the skillet. Heat to a boil. Reduce the heat to low. Cover and cook for 10 minutes or until the chicken is cooked through*.

The internal temperature of the chicken should reach 160°F.

Easy Chicken and Biscuits

MAKES: **5 SERVINGS**

START TO FINISH:
40 minutes

Prep: *10 minutes*
Cook: *30 minutes*

1 can (10¾ ounces) Campbell's® Condensed Cream of Celery Soup (Regular **or** 98% Fat Free)

1 can (10¾ ounces) Campbell's® Condensed Cream of Potato Soup

1 cup milk

¼ teaspoon dried thyme leaves, crushed

¼ teaspoon ground black pepper

4 cups cooked cut-up vegetables*

2 cups cubed cooked chicken

1 package (about 7 ounces) refrigerated buttermilk biscuits (10)

1. Stir the soups, milk, thyme, black pepper, vegetables and chicken in a 13×9×2-inch shallow baking dish.

2. Bake at 400°F. for 15 minutes. Stir.

3. Cut each biscuit into quarters. Arrange cut biscuits over the chicken mixture.

4. Bake for 15 minutes more or until the biscuits are golden.

*Use a combination of broccoli flowerets, cauliflower flowerets and carrots.

Chicken & Tortellini Stew

MAKES: **6 SERVINGS**

START TO FINISH:
45 minutes

Prep: *10 minutes*
Cook: *35 minutes*

- 1 **tablespoon cornstarch**
- 1 **tablespoon water**
- 2 **tablespoons vegetable oil**
- ¾ **pound skinless, boneless chicken breasts, cut into cubes**
- 1 **cup frozen sliced carrots**
- 1 **cup frozen cut green beans**
- ¾ **cup chopped onion**
- 6 **cups Swanson® Chicken Broth (Regular, Natural Goodness™ or Certified Organic)**
- 1 **cup dried cheese-filled tortellini**
- 2 **tablespoons chopped fresh parsley (optional)**

1. Stir the cornstarch and water in a small bowl. Set the mixture aside.

2. Heat **1 tablespoon** of the oil in a 4-quart saucepan over medium-high heat. Add the chicken and cook until it's well browned, stirring often. Remove the chicken with a slotted spoon and set aside.

3. Reduce the heat to medium and add the remaining oil. Add carrots, green beans and onion. Cook until the vegetables are tender-crisp.

4. Stir the broth into the saucepan. Heat to a boil. Return the chicken to the saucepan. Add the tortellini and parsley, if desired. Cook for 10 minutes or until tortellini is tender but still firm.

5. Stir the cornstarch mixture and stir it into the saucepan. Cook until the mixture boils and thickens slightly.

Cheesy Chicken and Rice Bake

Campbell's Kitchen Tip:
Stir **2 cups** of fresh, canned or frozen vegetables into the soup mixture before topping with chicken.

MAKES: **6 SERVINGS**

    1   can (10¾ ounces) Campbell's® Condensed
        Cream of Chicken Soup (Regular **or**
        98% Fat Free)
1⅓   cups water
    ¾   cup **uncooked** regular long-grain white
        rice
    ½   teaspoon onion powder
    ¼   teaspoon ground black pepper
    4   to 6 skinless, boneless chicken breast
        halves
    1   cup shredded Cheddar cheese (4 ounces)

1. Stir the soup, water, rice, onion powder and black pepper in a 12×8×2-inch shallow baking dish. Top with the chicken. Sprinkle the chicken with additional pepper. Cover the dish with foil.

2. Bake at 375°F. for 45 minutes or until the chicken is cooked through* and the rice is tender and most of the liquid is absorbed.

3. Uncover the dish. Sprinkle the cheese over the chicken.

*The internal temperature of the chicken should reach 160°F.

Chicken Florentine Lasagna

MAKES: **6 SERVINGS**

START TO FINISH:
1 hour, 15 minutes

Prep: *10 minutes*

Bake: *1 hour*

Stand: *5 minutes*

Time-Saving Tip:
To thaw spinach, microwave on HIGH for 3 minutes, breaking apart with a fork halfway through heating.

2 cans (10¾ ounces **each**) Campbell's® Condensed Cream of Chicken with Herbs Soup

2 cups milk

1 egg

1 container (15 ounces) ricotta cheese

6 **uncooked** lasagna noodles

1 package (about 10 ounces) frozen chopped spinach, thawed and well drained

2 cups cubed cooked chicken **or** turkey

2 cups shredded Cheddar cheese (8 ounces)

1. Stir the soup and milk in a medium bowl.

2. Stir the egg and ricotta cheese in another small bowl.

3. Spread **1 cup** of the soup mixture in a 13×9×2-inch shallow baking dish. Top with **3** noodles, the ricotta mixture, spinach, chicken, **1 cup** Cheddar cheese and **1 cup** soup mixture. Top with remaining **3** noodles and remaining soup mixture. Cover the dish with foil.

4. Bake at 375°F. for 1 hour. Uncover the dish and sprinkle with the remaining Cheddar cheese. Let the lasagna stand for 5 minutes before serving.

Chicken with White Beans

MAKES: **4 SERVINGS**

START TO FINISH:
50 minutes

Prep: *5 minutes*
Cook: *45 minutes*

- 1 tablespoon vegetable oil
- 4 bone-in chicken breast halves (about 2 pounds)*
- 2 cups Prego® Traditional Italian Sauce
- ¼ teaspoon garlic powder **or** 2 cloves garlic, minced
- 1 large onion, chopped (about 1 cup)
- 2 cans (about 16 ounces **each**) white kidney (cannellini) beans, rinsed and drained

1. Heat the oil in a 10-inch skillet over medium-high heat. Add the chicken and cook for 10 minutes or until it's well browned on both sides. Remove chicken and set aside.

2. Stir the Italian sauce, garlic powder, onion and beans into the skillet. Heat to a boil. Return the chicken to the skillet. Reduce the heat to low. Cover and cook for 30 minutes or until the chicken is cooked through**.

*If desired, remove skin from the chicken before browning.

**The internal temperature of the chicken should reach 170°F.

Citrus Chicken and Rice

MAKES: **6 SERVINGS**

START TO FINISH:
40 minutes

Prep: *5 minutes*

Cook: *35 minutes*

- 4 to 6 skinless, boneless chicken breast halves
- 1¾ cups Swanson® Chicken Broth (Regular, Natural Goodness™ **or** Certified Organic)
- ½ cup orange juice
- 1 medium onion, chopped (about ½ cup)
- 1 cup **uncooked** regular long-grain white rice
- 3 tablespoons chopped fresh parsley **or** 1 tablespoon dried parsley flakes
- Orange slices

1. Cook the chicken in a 10-inch nonstick skillet over medium-high heat for 10 minutes or until it's well browned on both sides. Remove the chicken and set aside.

2. Stir the broth, orange juice, onion and rice into the skillet. Heat to a boil. Reduce the heat to low. Cover and cook for 10 minutes.

3. Return the chicken to the skillet. Cover and cook for 10 minutes more or until chicken is cooked through*. Stir in parsley and top with orange slices.

*The internal temperature of the chicken should reach 160°F.

Cornbread Chicken Pot Pie

MAKES: **4 SERVINGS**

START TO FINISH:
35 minutes

Prep: *5 minutes*
Bake: *30 minutes*

- 1 can (10¾ ounces) Campbell's® Condensed Cream of Chicken Soup (Regular **or** 98% Fat Free)
- 1 can (about 8 ounces) whole kernel corn, drained
- 2 cups cubed cooked chicken **or** turkey
- 1 package (8½ ounces) corn muffin mix
- ¾ cup milk
- 1 egg
- ½ cup shredded Cheddar cheese (2 ounces)

1. Heat the oven to 400°F. Stir the soup, corn and chicken in a 9-inch pie plate.

2. Stir together the muffin mix, milk and egg with a fork in a small bowl until the ingredients are mixed. Spoon over the chicken mixture.

3. Bake for 30 minutes or until the cornbread is golden. Sprinkle with cheese.

Country Chicken Casserole

MAKES: **5 SERVINGS**

1 can (10¾ ounces) Campbell's® Condensed Cream of Celery Soup (Regular **or** 98% Fat Free)
1 can (10¾ ounces) Campbell's® Condensed Cream of Potato Soup
1 cup milk
¼ teaspoon dried thyme leaves, crushed
⅛ teaspoon ground black pepper
4 cups cooked cut-up vegetables*
2 cups cubed cooked chicken **or** turkey
1½ cups water
4 tablespoons butter
4 cups Pepperidge Farm® Herb Seasoned Stuffing

1. Stir the soups, milk, thyme, black pepper, vegetables and chicken in 13×9×2-inch shallow baking dish.

2. Heat the water and butter in 2-quart saucepan over high heat to a boil. Add the stuffing and stir lightly to coat. Spoon the stuffing over the chicken mixture.

3. Bake at 400°F. for 25 minutes or until hot.

Use a combination of cut green beans and sliced carrots.

Creamy Enchiladas Verde

MAKES: **4 SERVINGS**

START TO FINISH:
30 minutes

Prep: *10 minutes*
Bake: *20 minutes*

- 1 can (10¾ ounces) Campbell's® Condensed Creamy Chicken Verde Soup
- ½ teaspoon garlic powder
- 1½ cups chopped cooked chicken
- ⅔ cup shredded Cheddar **or** Monterey Jack cheese
- 8 corn tortillas (6-inch), warmed
- ¼ cup milk

1. Stir ½ **can** of the soup, garlic powder, chicken, and ⅓ **cup** of the cheese in a medium bowl.

2. Spoon **about** ⅓ **cup** of the chicken mixture down the center of each tortilla. Roll up the tortillas and place them seam-side down in 12×8×2-inch shallow baking dish.

3. Stir the remaining soup and milk in a small bowl and pour over the filled tortillas. Top with the remaining cheese.

4. Bake at 375°F. for 20 minutes or until the enchiladas are hot and bubbly.

Casseroles, One-Dish Meals and More   **83**

Country Chicken Stew

MAKES: **4 SERVINGS**

START TO FINISH:
40 minutes

Prep: *15 minutes*
Cook: *25 minutes*

2 slices bacon, diced

1 medium onion, sliced (about ½ cup)

1 can (10¾ ounces) Campbell's® Condensed Cream of Chicken Soup (Regular **or** 98% Fat Free)

1 soup can water

½ teaspoon dried oregano leaves, crushed

3 medium potatoes (about 1 pound), cut into 1-inch pieces

2 medium carrots, sliced (about 1 cup)

1 cup frozen cut green beans

2 cans (4.5 ounces **each**) Swanson® Premium Chunk Chicken Breast, drained

2 tablespoons chopped fresh parsley

1. Cook bacon in a 10-inch skillet over medium heat until it's crisp. Remove the bacon with a slotted spoon and drain it on paper towels.

2. Add the onion and cook in hot drippings until tender.

3. Stir the soup, water, oregano, potatoes and carrots into the skillet. Heat to a boil. Reduce the heat to low. Cover and cook for 15 minutes.

4. Stir in the beans. Cover and cook for 10 minutes more or until vegetables are tender. Stir in the bacon, chicken and parsley and cook until hot.

Creamy Pesto Chicken & Bow Ties

MAKES: **4 SERVINGS**

START TO FINISH:
20 minutes

Prep: *5 minutes*
Cook: *15 minutes*

- 2 tablespoons butter
- 1 pound skinless, boneless chicken breasts, cut into cubes
- 1 can (10¾ ounces) Campbell's® Condensed Cream of Chicken Soup (Regular **or** 98% Fat Free)
- ½ cup milk
- ½ cup prepared pesto sauce
- 3 cups bow tie-shaped pasta (farfalle), cooked and drained

1. Heat the butter in 10-inch skillet over medium-high heat. Add the chicken and cook until it's well browned, stirring often.

2. Stir the soup, milk and pesto sauce into the skillet. Heat to a boil. Reduce the heat to low. Cover and cook for 5 minutes or until the chicken is cooked through. Stir in the pasta. Cook until it's hot.

Chicken and Peppers Pie

START TO FINISH:
40 minutes

Prep: *10 minutes*
Cook: *30 minutes*

MAKES: **6 SERVINGS**

1 can (10¾ ounces) Campbell's® Condensed Cream of Chicken Soup (Regular **or** 98% Fat Free)
½ cup Pace® Picante Sauce
½ cup sour cream
2 teaspoons chili powder
1 jar (7 ounces) whole roasted sweet peppers, drained and cut into strips
4 medium green onions, sliced (about ½ cup)
3 cups cubed cooked chicken
1 package (11 ounces) refrigerated cornbread twists
Fresh sage leaves (optional)

1. Stir the soup, picante sauce, sour cream, chili powder, peppers, green onions and chicken in a 12×8×2-inch shallow baking dish.

2. Bake at 400°F. for 15 minutes. Stir.

3. Separate the bread twists into 16 strips. Arrange the strips, lattice-fashion, over the chicken mixture, overlapping strips as necessary to fit.

4. Bake for 15 minutes more or until the bread is golden. Top with sage, if desired.

Chicken & Stuffing Skillet

START TO FINISH:
25 minutes

Prep: *5 minutes*
Cook: *20 minutes*

MAKES: **6 SERVINGS**

   3 tablespoons butter
   4 to 6 skinless, boneless chicken breast halves
   1 box (6 ounces) Pepperidge Farm® One Step Chicken Flavored Stuffing Mix
1¼ cups water
   1 can (10¾ ounces) Campbell's® Condensed Cream of Chicken Soup (Regular **or** 98% Fat Free)
  ½ cup milk
  ½ cup shredded Cheddar cheese

1. Heat **1 tablespoon** butter in a 10-inch skillet over medium-high heat. Add the chicken and cook for 12 to 15 minutes or until the chicken is cooked through*. Remove the chicken and set it aside.

2. Prepare the stuffing in the skillet using the water and the remaining butter according to the package directions **except** let it stand for 2 minutes.

3. Return the chicken to the skillet and reduce the heat to medium. Stir the soup and milk in a small bowl and pour it over the chicken. Sprinkle with the cheese. Cover and cook until the mixture is hot and bubbling.

The internal temperature of the chicken should reach 160°F.

Chicken Dijon with Noodles

MAKES: **6 SERVINGS**

START TO FINISH:
25 minutes

Prep/Cook: *25 minutes*

2 tablespoons butter

4 to 6 skinless, boneless chicken breast halves

1 medium onion, chopped (about ½ cup)

1 can (10¾ ounces) Campbell's® Condensed Cream of Mushroom Soup (Regular **or** 98% Fat Free)

¼ cup apple juice **or** milk

1 tablespoon Dijon-style mustard

1 tablespoon chopped fresh parsley **or** 1 teaspoon dried parsley flakes

Hot cooked noodles

Leftover Tip:
Cut up leftover chicken and add back to leftover sauce. Cover and refrigerate. Reheat chicken mixture and serve over toast topped with some chopped apple.

1. Heat the butter in a 10-inch skillet over medium-high heat. Add the chicken and cook for 10 minutes or until it's well browned on both sides. Remove the chicken and set aside.

2. Reduce the heat to medium. Add the onion and cook until tender.

3. Stir the soup, apple juice, mustard and parsley into the skillet. Heat to a boil. Return the chicken to the skillet and reduce the heat to low. Cover and cook for 5 minutes or until the chicken is cooked through. Serve with the noodles.

Chicken Broccoli Divan

START TO FINISH:
55 minutes

Prep: *10 minutes*
Bake: *45 minutes*

MAKES: **8 SERVINGS**

8 cups fresh **or** frozen broccoli flowerets

8 skinless, boneless chicken breast halves

1 can (26 ounces) Campbell's® Condensed Cream of Chicken Soup

1¼ cups milk

1 cup shredded Cheddar cheese (4 ounces)

¼ cup dry bread crumbs

2 tablespoons butter, melted

1. Arrange the broccoli and chicken in a 4-quart shallow baking dish.

2. Stir the soup and milk in a small bowl and pour over the broccoli and chicken.

3. Sprinkle the cheese over the soup mixture. Mix the bread crumbs with the butter in a small bowl and sprinkle over the cheese.

4. Bake at 350°F. for 45 minutes or until chicken is cooked through.

Chicken Asparagus Gratin

MAKES: **4 SERVINGS**

START TO FINISH:
50 minutes

Prep: *20 minutes*
Bake: *30 minutes*

- 1 can (10¾ ounces) Campbell's® Condensed Cream of Asparagus Soup
- ½ cup milk
- ¼ teaspoon onion powder
- ⅛ teaspoon ground black pepper
- 1½ cups cooked cut asparagus
- 1½ cups cubed cooked chicken
- 3 cups cooked corkscrew-shaped pasta
- 1 cup shredded Cheddar **or** Swiss cheese (4 ounces)

1. Stir the soup, milk, onion powder, black pepper, asparagus, chicken, pasta and ½ **cup** of the cheese in a 12×8×2-inch shallow baking dish.

2. Bake at 400°F. for 25 minutes or until hot. Stir.

3. Sprinkle with the remaining cheese. Bake for 5 minutes more or until the cheese melts.

Timeout Roast Chicken with Ham Sauce

START TO FINISH:
1 hour, 10 minutes

Prep: *10 minutes*

Bake: *1 hour*

MAKES: **4 SERVINGS**

- 4 bone-in chicken breasts (about 2 pounds)
- 4 ounces sliced prosciutto **or** cooked ham, cut into very thin strips
- 1 can (10¾ ounces) Campbell's® Condensed Cream of Mushroom Soup (Regular **or** 98% Fat Free)
- 1 container (8 ounces) sour cream
- 1 teaspoon onion powder
- ½ teaspoon garlic powder
- ¼ teaspoon paprika
- ¼ teaspoon ground black pepper
- 4 hot baked potatoes, split **or** 4 servings mashed potatoes
- Fresh parsley sprigs for garnish

1. Put the chicken in a 13×9×2-inch shallow baking dish and bake at 375°F. for 30 minutes. Pour off any fat.

2. Put the prosciutto in the dish around the chicken. Stir the soup, sour cream, onion powder, garlic powder, paprika and black pepper in a small bowl. Spoon over the chicken and bake for 30 minutes more or until the chicken is cooked through*. Remove the chicken to a serving platter. Stir the sauce and serve with the chicken and potatoes. Garnish with the parsley.

*The internal temperature of the chicken should reach 170°F.

Orange Chicken with Green Onions and Walnuts

START TO FINISH:
*8 to 9 hours,
10 minutes*

Prep: *10 minutes*
Cook: *8 to 9 hours*

MAKES: **8 SERVINGS**

2	tablespoons cornstarch
1½	cups Swanson® Chicken Broth (Regular, Natural Goodness™ **or** Certified Organic)
¼	cup teriyaki sauce
3	cloves garlic, minced
¾	cup orange marmalade
4	medium green onions, sliced (about ½ cup)
8	skinless chicken thighs (about 2 pounds)
½	cup walnut pieces
	Hot cooked rice

1. Stir the cornstarch, broth, teriyaki sauce, garlic, marmalade and ¼ **cup** green onions in a 6-quart slow cooker. Add the chicken and turn to coat with the broth mixture.

2. Cover and cook on LOW for 8 to 9 hours* or until chicken is cooked through. Sprinkle with walnuts and remaining green onions before serving. Serve with rice.

*Or on HIGH for 4 to 5 hours

Slow-Simmered Chicken Rice Soup

MAKES: **8 SERVINGS**

START TO FINISH:
7 to 8 hours,
15 minutes

Prep: *15 minutes*

Cook: *7 to 8 hours*

- ½ cup **uncooked** wild rice
- ½ cup **uncooked** regular long-grain white rice
- 1 tablespoon vegetable oil
- 5¼ cups Swanson® Chicken Broth (Regular, Natural Goodness™ **or** Certified Organic)
- 2 teaspoons dried thyme leaves, crushed
- ¼ teaspoon crushed red pepper
- 2 stalks celery, coarsely chopped (about 1 cup)
- 1 medium onion, chopped (about ½ cup)
- 1 pound skinless, boneless chicken breasts, cut into cubes

  Sour cream (optional)

  Chopped green onions (optional)

1. Stir the wild rice, white rice and oil in a 3½-quart slow cooker. Cover and cook on HIGH for 15 minutes.

2. Stir the broth, thyme, red pepper, celery, onion and chicken into the cooker. Turn the heat to LOW. Cover and cook on LOW for 7 to 8 hours* or until the chicken is cooked through.

3. Serve with the sour cream and green onions, if desired.

*Or on HIGH for 4 to 5 hours

Chicken & Roasted Garlic Risotto

MAKES: **6 SERVINGS**

Easy Substitution Tip:
For flavor variation, use 1 cup frozen peas and pearl onions or frozen mixed vegetables for the 1 cup frozen peas and carrots.

- 4 to 6 skinless, boneless chicken breast halves
- 1 tablespoon butter
- 1 can (10¾ ounces) Campbell's® Condensed Cream of Chicken Soup (Regular **or** 98% Fat Free)
- 1 can (10¾ ounces) Campbell's® Condensed Cream of Mushroom with Roasted Garlic Soup
- 2 cups water
- 2 cups **uncooked** instant white rice
- 1 cup frozen peas and carrots

1. Season chicken as desired.

2. Heat the butter in a 10-inch skillet over medium-high heat. Add the chicken and cook for 10 minutes or until it's well browned on both sides. Remove the chicken and set aside.

3. Stir the soups and water into the skillet. Heat to a boil. Stir in the rice and vegetables. Return the chicken to the skillet and reduce the heat to low. Cover and cook for 5 minutes or until the chicken is cooked through*. Remove the skillet from the heat. Let stand for 5 minutes.

*The internal temperature of the chicken should reach 160°F.

Extra Point Enchilada-Style Casserole

START TO FINISH:
45 minutes

Prep: *10 minutes*
Bake: *35 minutes*

MAKES: **8 SERVINGS**

2 cans (10¾ ounces **each**) Campbell's®
   Condensed Cheddar Cheese Soup
½ cup water
1 jar (16 ounces) Pace® Chunky Salsa
4 cups cubed cooked chicken
8 flour **or** 12 corn tortillas (6- to 8-inch), cut
   into strips
1 cup shredded Cheddar cheese (4 ounces)

1. Stir the soup, water, ½ **cup** of the salsa and chicken in a large bowl. Stir in the tortillas. Spread the chicken mixture in a 13×9×2-inch shallow baking dish. Top with the cheese. Cover the dish with foil.

2. Bake at 350°F. for 35 minutes or until hot and bubbly. Serve with the remaining salsa.

Tantalizing TURKEY

IDEAS FOR USING TURKEY AND TURKEY LEFTOVERS

Porcupine Meatballs

MAKES: **5 SERVINGS**

START TO FINISH:
35 minutes

Prep: *15 minutes*
Cook: *20 minutes*

1 pound ground turkey
2 cups cooked brown **or** regular long-grain white rice
1 egg
¾ teaspoon dried oregano leaves, crushed
½ teaspoon garlic powder
¼ teaspoon ground black pepper
1 jar (1 pound 10 ounces) Prego® Traditional **or** Tomato, Basil & Garlic Italian Sauce

1. Thoroughly mix the turkey, rice, egg, oregano, garlic powder and black pepper in a medium bowl.

2. Shape the mixture into 25 meatballs.

3. Heat the Italian sauce in a 12-inch skillet over medium-high heat. Add the meatballs in one layer. Heat to a boil. Reduce the heat to low. Cover and cook for 10 minutes or until meatballs are cooked through*.

*The internal temperature of the meatballs should reach 160°F.

Black Bean, Corn & Turkey Chili

START TO FINISH:
55 minutes

Prep: *15 minutes*

Cook: *40 minutes*

MAKES: **6 SERVINGS**

1 tablespoon vegetable oil

1 pound ground turkey

1 large onion, chopped (about 1 cup)

2 tablespoons chili powder

1 teaspoon ground cumin

1 teaspoon dried oregano leaves, crushed

½ teaspoon ground black pepper

¼ teaspoon garlic powder **or** 2 cloves garlic, minced

1¾ cups Swanson® Chicken Broth (Regular, Natural Goodness™ **or** Certified Organic)

1 cup Pace® Chunky Salsa

1 tablespoon sugar

1 can (about 16 ounces) black beans, rinsed and drained

1 can (16 ounces) whole kernel corn, drained

1. Heat the oil in a 4-quart saucepan over medium-high heat. Add the turkey, onion, chili powder, cumin, oregano, black pepper and garlic powder. Cook until the turkey is well browned, stirring frequently to break up meat.

2. Stir the broth, salsa, sugar, beans and corn into the saucepan. Heat to a boil. Reduce the heat to low. Cover and cook for 30 minutes.

Creamy Turkey & Pasta Casserole

MAKES: **4 SERVINGS**

1 can (10¾ ounces) Campbell's® Condensed Cream of Mushroom Soup (Regular **or** 98% Fat Free)

½ cup sour cream

2 medium green onions, chopped (about ¼ cup)

2 cups cubed cooked turkey **or** chicken

1 cup elbow macaroni, cooked and drained

2 tablespoons Italian-seasoned dry bread crumbs

1 tablespoon grated Parmesan cheese

1 tablespoon butter, melted

1. Stir the soup, sour cream, green onions, turkey and macaroni in a 1½-quart casserole.

2. Bake at 350°F. for 20 minutes or until hot. Stir.

3. Mix the bread crumbs, cheese and butter in a small bowl and sprinkle over the turkey mixture. Bake for 5 minutes more or until the topping is golden brown.

Lemon-Basil Turkey with Roasted Vegetables

START TO FINISH:
1 hour, 50 minutes

Prep: *20 minutes*

Bake: *1 hour,*
30 minutes

Time-Saving Tip:
To quickly peel the onions, put the onions in a medium bowl. Pour boiling water over them. Let stand for 5 minutes. Drain and then slip off the skins.

MAKES: **8 SERVINGS**

	Vegetable cooking spray
2	medium lemons
	8-pound fresh turkey breast*
24	baby Yukon gold potatoes
1	butternut squash (about 1¼ pounds), peeled, seeded and cut into 1-inch cubes (about 3 cups)
8	medium beets, peeled and cut into 1-inch cubes (3¾ cups)
12	small white onions, peeled **or** 1 cup frozen small whole onions
1	tablespoon butter, melted
1	tablespoon dried basil leaves, crushed
1	cup Swanson® Chicken Broth (Regular, Natural Goodness™ **or** Certified Organic)

1. Spray a 17×11-inch roasting pan with cooking spray.

2. Cut **1** lemon into thin slices. Squeeze **2 tablespoons** juice from remaining lemon. Loosen skin on turkey breast and place lemon slices under the skin.

3. Place the turkey, (meat-side up), potatoes, squash, beets and onions in the prepared pan. Brush the turkey with butter and sprinkle with basil. Insert a meat thermometer into the thickest part of the meat, making sure the thermometer is not touching the bone.

4. Stir the broth and lemon juice in a small bowl. Pour **half** of the broth mixture over the turkey and vegetables.

5. Roast the turkey at 375°F. for 1 hour. Stir the vegetables.

6. Add the remaining broth mixture to the pan. Roast for 30 minutes more or until the thermometer reaches 170°F.

If using a frozen turkey breast, thaw before cooking.

Herbed Turkey Breast

MAKES: **8 SERVINGS**

START TO FINISH:
*8 to 9 hours,
20 minutes*

Prep: *10 minutes*

Cook: *8 to 9 hours*

Stand: *10 minutes*

1 can (10¾ ounces) Campbell's® Condensed Cream of Mushroom Soup (Regular **or** 98% Fat Free)

½ cup water

4½- to 5-pound fresh turkey breast*

1 teaspoon poultry seasoning

1 tablespoon chopped fresh parsley

Hot mashed potatoes

1. Stir the soup and water in a 3½-to 6-quart slow cooker. Rinse the turkey with cold water and pat dry with a paper towel. Rub turkey with poultry seasoning and place meat-side up in cooker. Sprinkle with the parsley.

2. Cover and cook on LOW for 8 to 9 hours**. Insert a meat thermometer into the thickest part of the meat, making sure the thermometer is not touching the bone and the temperature should reach 170°F. Let the turkey stand for 10 minutes before slicing. Serve with the potatoes.

If using a frozen turkey breast, thaw before cooking.

**Or on HIGH 4 to 5 hours*

Smoked Turkey & Broccoli Gratin

MAKES: **4 SERVINGS**

START TO FINISH:
35 minutes

Prep: *5 minutes*
Bake: *30 minutes*

- 1 can (10¾ ounces) Campbell's® Condensed Cheddar Cheese Soup
- ½ cup milk
- 1 tablespoon Dijon-style mustard
- 1 package (20 ounces) frozen chopped broccoli, thawed and drained (4 cups)
- 1 pound cooked smoked turkey, cubed (about 3 cups)
- 1 cup small shell pasta, cooked and drained
- 2 tablespoons dry bread crumbs
- 1 tablespoon butter, melted

1. Stir the soup, milk, mustard, broccoli, turkey and pasta in a 12×8×2-inch shallow baking dish. Mix the bread crumbs with the butter in a small cup. Sprinkle the bread crumb mixture over the turkey mixture.

2. Bake at 375°F. for 30 minutes or until hot and bubbly.

Tantalizing
TURKEY

Tuscan Turkey & Beans

MAKES: **4 SERVINGS**

2 tablespoons olive **or** vegetable oil
4 turkey breast cutlets **or** slices (about 1 pound)
1 medium onion, chopped (about ½ cup)
2 cloves garlic, minced
1½ teaspoons Italian seasoning, crushed
1 can (about 14½ ounces) diced tomatoes, undrained
1½ cups packed chopped fresh spinach leaves
1 can (10¾ ounces) Campbell's® Condensed Cream of Celery Soup (Regular **or** 98% Fat Free)
¼ teaspoon ground black pepper
1 can (about 15 ounces) white kidney (cannellini) beans, rinsed and drained
Grated Parmesan cheese

1. Heat **1 tablespoon** of the oil in a 12-inch skillet over medium heat. Add the turkey in 2 batches and cook for 3 minutes or until the turkey is lightly browned on both sides. Remove the turkey and keep it warm.

2. Reduce the heat to medium and add the remaining oil. Add the onion, garlic and Italian seasoning. Cook and stir until the onion is tender-crisp, stirring often.

3. Add the tomatoes and spinach and cook just until the spinach wilts, stirring occasionally.

4. Stir the soup, black pepper and beans into the skillet. Heat to a boil. Return the turkey to the skillet and reduce the heat to low. Cover and cook for 5 minutes or until the turkey is cooked through*. Sprinkle with the cheese.

*The internal temperature of the turkey should reach 160°F.

Turkey Apple Cranberry Bake

START TO FINISH:
50 minutes

Prep: *20 minutes*
Bake: *30 minutes*

MAKES: **4 SERVINGS**

1 cup Pepperidge Farm® Herbed Seasoned Stuffing
1 tablespoon butter, melted
1 can (10¾ ounces) Campbell's® Condensed Cream of Celery Soup (Regular **or** 98% Fat Free)
½ cup milk
2 cups cubed cooked turkey
1 medium apple, diced (about 1½ cups)
1 stalk celery, finely chopped (about ½ cup)
½ cup dried cranberries
½ cup pecan halves, chopped

1. Stir the stuffing and butter in a small bowl. Set aside.

2. Stir the soup, milk, turkey, apple, celery, cranberries and pecans in a 12×8×2-inch shallow baking dish. Sprinkle the reserved stuffing mixture over the turkey mixture.

3. Bake at 400°F. for 30 minutes or until hot and bubbly.

Turkey Broccoli Alfredo

START TO FINISH:
15 minutes

Prep/Cook: *15 minutes*

Easy Substitution Tip:
Substitute spaghetti for linguine and cooked chicken for the turkey.

MAKES: **4 SERVINGS**

½ of a 16 ounce package linguine
1 cup fresh **or** frozen broccoli flowerets
1 can (10¾ ounces) Campbell's® Condensed Cream of Mushroom Soup (Regular **or** 98% Fat Free)
½ cup milk
½ cup grated Parmesan cheese
¼ teaspoon ground black pepper
2 cups cubed cooked turkey

1. Prepare the linguine according to the package directions in a 3-quart saucepan. Add the broccoli for the last 4 minutes of the cooking time. Drain the linguine and broccoli well in a colander. Return them to the saucepan.

2. Stir the soup, milk, cheese, black pepper and turkey into the linguine and broccoli. Cook and stir over medium heat until hot and bubbling. Serve with additional Parmesan cheese.

112 *Casseroles, One-Dish Meals and More*

Turkey Cutlets with Stuffing & Cranberry

MAKES: **8 SERVINGS**

START TO FINISH:
1 hour, 20 minutes

Prep: *15 minutes*

Bake: *1 hour, 5 minutes*

- 1 bag (14 ounces) Pepperidge Farm® Cubed Herb Seasoned Stuffing
- 1 stick (½ cup) butter
- 1 stalk celery, chopped (about ½ cup)
- 1 medium onion, chopped (about ½ cup)
- 1¾ cups Swanson® Chicken Broth (Regular, Natural Goodness™ **or** Certified Organic)
- 1 can (16 ounces) whole cranberry sauce
- 8 turkey breast cutlets **or** slices (about 2 pounds)
- 1 can (10¾ ounces) Campbell's® Condensed Cream of Chicken Soup (Regular **or** 98% Fat Free)
- ⅓ cup milk

Easy Substitution Tip:
Substitute a whole turkey London broil (about 2 pounds) and cut it into 8 cutlets for the packaged turkey cutlets.

1. Coarsely crush some of the stuffing to make **1 cup** stuffing crumbs. Set aside.

2. Heat the butter in 4-quart saucepan over medium heat. Add the celery and onion and cook until they're tender.

3. Stir the broth into the saucepan. Heat to a boil. Remove from the heat. Add the remaining stuffing and stir lightly to coat.

4. Spoon the stuffing mixture into a 13×9×2-inch baking pan. Spread the cranberry sauce over the stuffing. Top with the turkey.

5. Stir the soup and milk in a small bowl. Pour over the turkey. Sprinkle with the reserved stuffing crumbs.

6. Bake at 375°F. for 1 hour, 5 minutes or until turkey is cooked through*.

*The internal temperature of the turkey should reach 160°F.

Turkey Stuffing Divan

MAKES: **6 SERVINGS**

START TO FINISH:
40 minutes

Prep: *10 minutes*
Bake: *30 minutes*

Easy Substitution Tip:
For **2 cups** cooked broccoli cuts use about **1 pound** fresh broccoli, trimmed and cut into 1-inch pieces (about 2 cups) **or 1 package** (10 ounces) frozen broccoli cuts.

4 cups Pepperidge Farm® Herb Seasoned Stuffing
1¼ cups water
4 tablespoons butter
2 cups cooked broccoli cuts
2 cups cubed cooked turkey **or** chicken
1 can (10¾ ounces) Campbell's® Condensed Cream of Celery Soup (Regular **or** 98% Fat Free)
½ cup milk
1 cup shredded Cheddar cheese (4 ounces)

1. Prepare the stuffing using the water and butter according to the package directions.

2. Spoon the stuffing into a 12×8×2-inch shallow baking dish. Arrange the broccoli and turkey over the stuffing mixture.

3. Stir the soup, milk and ½ **cup** of the cheese in a small bowl. Pour over the turkey mixture. Sprinkle with the remaining cheese.

4. Bake at 350°F. for 30 minutes or until hot.

Southern Cornbread Turkey Pot Pie

MAKES: **4 SERVINGS**

1 can (10¾ ounces) Campbell's® Condensed Cream of Chicken Soup (Regular **or** 98% Fat Free)

⅛ teaspoon ground black pepper

2 cups cubed cooked turkey

1 can (about 8 ounces) whole kernel corn, drained

1 package (11 ounces) refrigerated cornbread twists

1. Heat the oven to 425°F.

2. Stir the soup, black pepper, turkey and corn in a 2-quart saucepan over medium heat. Cook and stir until it's hot. Pour the turkey mixture into a 9-inch pie plate.

3. Separate cornbread into 8 pieces along perforations. (Do not unroll dough.) Place over hot turkey mixture.

4. Bake for 15 minutes or until cornbread is golden.

START TO FINISH:
25 minutes

Prep: *10 minutes*
Bake: *15 minutes*

Easy Substitution Tip:
Substitute cooked chicken for the turkey.

Fabulous
SEAFOOD

EASY DISHES USING FISH AND SHELLFISH

Tuna Noodle Casserole

START TO FINISH:
32 minutes

Prep: *10 minutes*

Cook: *22 minutes*

Easy Substitution Tip:
Substitute your family's favorite frozen vegetable for the peas.

MAKES: **4 SERVINGS**

- 1 can (10¾ ounces) Campbell's® Condensed Cream of Mushroom Soup (Regular **or** 98% Fat Free)
- ½ cup milk
- 1 cup frozen peas
- 2 cans (about 6 ounces **each**) tuna, drained and flaked
- 2 cups hot cooked medium egg noodles
- ½ cup shredded Cheddar cheese

1. Stir the soup, milk, peas, tuna and noodles in a 1½-quart casserole.

2. Bake at 400°F. for 20 minutes or until hot. Stir.

3. Sprinkle cheese over the tuna mixture. Bake for 2 minutes more or until the cheese melts.

Italian Fish Fillets

MAKES: **8 SERVINGS**

Easy Substitution Tip:
Substitute about
2 pounds firm white fish
fillets such as cod,
haddock or halibut for
the tilapia fillets.

 2 slices Pepperidge Farm® Sandwich White
    Bread, torn into pieces
 ⅓ cup shredded Parmesan cheese
 1 clove garlic
 ½ teaspoon dried thyme leaves, crushed
 ⅛ teaspoon ground black pepper
 2 tablespoons olive oil
 8 fresh tilapia fish fillets (3 to 4 ounces **each**)
 1 egg, beaten

1. Place the bread, cheese, garlic, thyme and black
pepper in an electric blender container. Cover and
blend until fine crumbs form. Slowly add the olive oil
and blend until moistened.

2. Put the fish fillets in a 17×11-inch roasting pan.
Brush with the egg. Divide the bread crumb mixture
evenly over the fillets.

3. Bake at 400°F. for 10 minutes or until the fish
flakes easily when tested with a fork and the crumb
topping is golden.

Garlic Shrimp & Broccoli with Pasta

MAKES: **6 SERVINGS**

START TO FINISH:
45 minutes

Prep: *15 minutes*
Bake: *30 minutes*

1 package (21.7 ounces) Campbell's® Supper Bakes® Garlic Chicken with Pasta (includes seasoning, pasta, baking sauce and crumb topping)

2¼ cups hot water

2 tablespoons butter, cut up

2 cups fresh **or** frozen broccoli flowerets

1½ pounds fresh large shrimp, peeled and deveined

1. Heat the oven to 400°F.

2. Mix the seasoning, hot water, butter, pasta and broccoli in a 13×9×2-inch shallow baking dish. Top with the shrimp.

3. Pour the baking sauce over the shrimp and pasta mixture. Cover the dish with foil.

4. Bake for 20 minutes. Uncover the dish and stir the pasta around the edge of dish. Sprinkle the crumb topping over the shrimp. Bake uncovered for 10 minutes more or until the shrimp turn pink and the pasta is tender. Stir the pasta before serving.

Crab & Asparagus Risotto

MAKES: **8 SERVINGS**

Campbell's Kitchen Tip:
Try some light or heavy cream to stir in with the Parmesan cheese for a creamier dish. Use about 2 tablespoons of it.

2 tablespoons olive oil
1 medium orange pepper, diced (about 1 cup)
½ cup chopped onion **or** shallots
2 cups **uncooked** Arborio rice (short-grain)
½ cup dry white wine
6 cups Swanson® Chicken Broth (Regular, Natural Goodness™ **or** Certified Organic), heated
½ pound asparagus or green beans, trimmed, cut into 1-inch pieces (about 1½ cups)
½ pound refrigerated pasteurized crabmeat (about 1½ cups)
¼ cup grated Parmesan cheese

1. Heat the oil in a 4-quart saucepan over medium heat. Add the pepper and onion and cook for 3 minutes or until the vegetables are tender. Add the rice and cook and stir for 2 minutes or until the rice is opaque.

2. Add the wine and cook and stir until it's absorbed. Stir **2 cups** of the hot broth into the rice mixture. Cook and stir until the broth is absorbed, maintaining the rice at a gentle simmer. Continue cooking and adding broth, ½ **cup** at a time, stirring until it's absorbed after each addition before adding more. Add the asparagus and crabmeat with the last broth addition.

3. Stir the cheese into the risotto. Remove the saucepan from the heat. Cover and let it stand for 5 minutes. Serve the risotto with additional cheese.

20-Minute Seafood Stew

MAKES: **4 SERVINGS**

Campbell's Kitchen Tip:
Before cooking, discard
any clams that remain
open when tapped.

2   cups Prego® Traditional Italian Sauce
1   bottle (8 fluid ounces) clam juice
¼   cup Burgundy **or** other dry red wine
     (optional)
1   pound fish **and/or** shellfish*
8   small clams in shells, well scrubbed
     Chopped fresh parsley

1. Heat the Italian sauce, clam juice and wine in a 3-quart saucepan over high heat to a boil. Reduce the heat to low. Cook for 5 minutes.

2. Stir the fish and clams into the saucepan. Cover and cook for 5 minutes more or until the fish flakes easily when tested with a fork and clams are open. Discard any clams that do not open. Sprinkle with parsley.

*Use any one **or** a combination of the following: Firm white fresh fish fillets (cut into 2-inch pieces), boneless fresh fish steaks (cut into 1-inch cubes), medium shrimp (shelled and deveined) **and/or** scallops.*

Jambalaya

MAKES: **6 SERVINGS**

START TO FINISH:
7 to 8 hours,
55 minutes

Prep: *15 minutes*
Cook: *7 to 8 hours,*
40 minutes

 2 cups Swanson® Chicken Broth (Regular, Natural Goodness™ **or** Certified Organic)
 1 tablespoon Creole seasoning
 1 large green pepper, diced (about 1⅓ cups)
 1 large onion, diced (about 1 cup)
 2 celery stalks, diced (about 1 cup)
 1 can (about 14½ ounces) diced tomatoes
 1 pound kielbasa, diced
 ¾ pound skinless, boneless chicken thighs, cut into cubes
 1 cup **uncooked** regular long-grain white rice
 ½ pound fresh medium shrimp, shelled and deveined

1. Stir the broth, Creole seasoning, pepper, onion, celery, tomatoes, kielbasa, chicken and rice in a 3½- to 6-quart slow cooker.

2. Cover and cook on LOW for 7 to 8 hours*.

3. Stir in the shrimp. Cover and cook for 40 minutes more or until chicken is cooked through and shrimp turn pink.

*Or on HIGH for 4 to 5 hours

New Orleans Shrimp Toss

START TO FINISH:
25 minutes

Prep: *10 minutes*

Cook: *15 minutes*

MAKES: **4 SERVINGS**

2 tablespoons vegetable oil

2 tablespoons lemon juice

1 tablespoon Worcestershire sauce

1 teaspoon Cajun seasoning

1 pound **uncooked** large shrimp, shelled and deveined

1 medium onion, chopped (about ½ cup)

2 cloves garlic, minced

1 can (10¾ ounces) Campbell's® Condensed Cream of Chicken with Herbs Soup

½ cup milk

1 teaspoon paprika

    Cornbread **or** biscuits

2 tablespoons chopped fresh chives, optional

1. Stir **1 tablespoon** of the oil, lemon juice, Worcestershire and Cajun seasoning in a medium bowl. Add the shrimp and toss lightly to coat.

2. Heat the remaining oil in a 10-inch skillet over medium-high heat. Add the onion and garlic. Cook and stir until the onion is tender.

3. Stir the soup, milk and paprika into the skillet. Heat to a boil. Add the shrimp mixture to the skillet and reduce the heat to low. Cover and cook for 5 minutes or until the shrimp turn pink. Serve with the cornbread and sprinkle with the chives, if desired.

Shrimp Stuffing au Gratin

MAKES: **6 SERVINGS**

4½ cups Pepperidge Farm® Herb Seasoned
      Stuffing
  3 tablespoons butter, melted
1¼ cups water
  2 cups cooked broccoli flowerets
  2 cups cooked medium shrimp
  1 can (10¾ ounces) Campbell's® Condensed
      Cream of Mushroom Soup (Regular **or**
      98% Fat Free)
 ½ cup milk
  2 tablespoons diced pimiento (optional)
  1 cup shredded Swiss cheese (4 ounces)

1. Coarsely crush ½ **cup** of the stuffing. Mix with **1 tablespoon** of the butter in a small cup. Set aside.

2. Stir water and remaining butter in a 12×8×2-inch shallow baking dish. Add the remaining stuffing and stir lightly to coat.

3. Arrange the broccoli and shrimp over the stuffing.

4. Stir the soup, milk, pimiento, if desired, and cheese in a small bowl. Pour the soup mixture over the shrimp mixture. Sprinkle with the reserved stuffing mixture.

5. Bake at 350°F. for 30 minutes or until hot.

START TO FINISH:
45 minutes

Prep: *15 minutes*
Bake: *30 minutes*

Campbell's Kitchen Tip:
You'll need to purchase 1 pound of fresh medium shrimp to have enough for 2 cups of cooked shrimp needed for this recipe. Heat 4 cups water in a 2-quart saucepan over high heat to a boil. Add the shrimp and cook for 1 to 3 minutes or until the shrimp turn pink. Drain in colander and rinse under cold water. Remove the shells and devein the shrimp.

Shrimp & Corn Chowder with Sun-Dried Tomatoes

START TO FINISH:
25 minutes

Prep: *5 minutes*

Cook: *20 minutes*

Easy Substitution Tip:
Substitute skim milk for the half-and-half.

MAKES: **4 SERVINGS**

1 can (10¾ ounces) Campbell's® Condensed Cream of Potato Soup

1½ cups half-and-half

2 cups whole kernel corn

2 tablespoons sun-dried tomatoes, cut in strips

1 cup small **or** medium cooked shrimp

2 tablespoons chopped fresh chives

Ground black **or** ground red pepper

1. Heat the soup, half-and-half, corn and tomatoes in a 2-quart saucepan over medium heat to a boil. Reduce the heat to low. Cover and cook for 10 minutes.

2. Stir in the shrimp. Sprinkle with chives. Cook until it's hot. Season to taste with black pepper.

Seafood Pot Pie

MAKES: **4 SERVINGS**

- ½ of a 17.3 ounce package Pepperidge Farm® Frozen Puff Pastry Sheet (1 sheet)
- 1 can (10¾ ounces) Campbell's® Condensed Cream of Onion Soup
- 1 can (10¾ ounces) Campbell's® Condensed New England Clam Chowder
- ⅛ teaspoon hot pepper sauce
- 1 package (10 ounces) frozen mixed vegetables, thawed
- 1 bag (12 ounces) frozen cooked baby shrimp, thawed (about 3 cups)
- 6 ounces imitation crabmeat (surimi), (about 1¼ cups)

START TO FINISH:
1 hour, 35 minutes

Thaw: *40 minutes*

Prep: *10 minutes*

Bake: *40 minutes*

Stand: *5 minutes*

1. Thaw the pastry sheet at room temperature for 40 minutes or until it's easy to handle. Heat the oven to 375°F. Lightly grease a 1½-quart shallow baking dish.

2. Stir the soups, hot sauce, vegetables, shrimp and crab in the prepared dish.

3. Unfold the pastry sheet on a lightly floured surface. Roll out to a 10×9-inch rectangle. Gently roll the pastry onto the rolling pin so that you can lift it and gently roll it onto the baking dish. Crimp or roll the edges to seal it to the dish.

4. Bake for 40 minutes or until the pastry is golden brown and the filling is bubbly. Let the pot pie stand for 5 minutes before serving.

Simple Special Seafood Chowder

MAKES: **6 SERVINGS**

1 tablespoon olive **or** vegetable oil

1 medium bulb fennel, trimmed, cut in half and thinly sliced (about 2 cups)

1 medium onion, chopped (about ½ cup)

1 teaspoon dried thyme leaves, crushed

5 cups water

1¾ cups Swanson® Vegetable Broth (Regular **or** Certified Organic)

1 can (10¾ ounces) Campbell's® Condensed Tomato Soup

1 package (10 ounces) frozen baby whole carrots, thawed (about 1½ cups)

½ pound fresh **or** thawed frozen firm white fish fillets (cod, haddock **or** halibut), cut into 2-inch pieces

½ pound fresh large shrimp, shelled and deveined

¾ pound mussels (about 12), well scrubbed

Freshly ground black pepper

1. Heat the oil in a 4-quart saucepan over medium heat. Add the fennel, onion and thyme and cook until the vegetables are tender. Stir in the water, broth, soup and carrots and heat to a boil.

2. Stir in the fish. Cook for 2 minutes. Stir in the shrimp and mussels. Cover and reduce the heat to low. Cook for 3 minutes more or until the fish flakes easily when tested with a fork, the shrimp turn pink and the mussels open. Discard any mussels that do not open. Serve the soup with black pepper.

Seafood Tomato Alfredo

MAKES: **4 SERVINGS**

START TO FINISH:
25 minutes

Prep: *5 minutes*

Cook: *20 minutes*

1   tablespoon butter

1   medium onion, chopped (about ½ cup)

1   can (10¾ ounces) Campbell's® Condensed Cream of Mushroom with Roasted Garlic Soup

½ cup milk

1   cup diced canned tomatoes

1   pound fresh fish fillets (flounder, haddock **or** halibut), cut into 2-inch pieces

Hot cooked linguine

1. Heat the butter in a 10-inch skillet over medium heat. Add the onion and cook until it's tender.

2. Stir the soup, milk and tomatoes into the skillet. Heat to a boil. Add the fish to the skillet and reduce the heat to low. Cover and cook for 10 minutes or until the fish flakes easily when tested with a fork.

3. Serve over the linguine.

Linguine with Easy Red Clam Sauce

MAKES: **4 SERVINGS**

START TO FINISH:
25 minutes

Prep: *10 minutes*
Cook: *15 minutes*

1   tablespoon olive **or** vegetable oil
2   cloves garlic, minced
1½ cups Prego® Traditional Italian Sauce
¼   cup Chablis **or** other dry white wine
1   tablespoon chopped fresh parsley
2   cans (6½ ounces **each**) minced clams, undrained
½   of a 16 ounce package linguine, cooked and drained
      Grated Parmesan cheese (optional)

1. Heat the oil in a 2-quart saucepan over medium heat. Add the garlic. Cook and stir until it's tender.

2. Stir the Italian sauce, wine, parsley and clams into the saucepan. Reduce the heat to low. Cover and cook for 10 minutes, stirring occasionally.

3. Serve the clam sauce over the linguine topped with the Parmesan cheese, if desired.

Poached Halibut with Pineapple Salsa

START TO FINISH:
25 minutes

Prep: *10 minutes*
Cook: *15 minutes*

MAKES: **4 SERVINGS**

1 can (15¼ ounces) pineapple chunks in
    juice, undrained
1 seedless cucumber, peeled and diced
    (about 1⅔ cups)
1 medium red pepper, chopped (about ¾ cup)
2 tablespoons chopped red onion
1 teaspoon white wine vinegar
1 teaspoon hot pepper sauce (optional)
1¾ cups Swanson® Chicken Broth (Regular,
    Natural Goodness™ **or** Certified Organic)
¼ cup white wine
4 fresh halibut fillets (about 1½ pounds)

1. Drain the pineapple and reserve ⅔ **cup** juice.

2. Stir the pineapple chunks, cucumber, red
pepper, red onion, vinegar and hot pepper sauce,
if desired, in a medium bowl and set aside.

3. Heat the broth, wine and reserved pineapple
juice in a 12-inch skillet over high heat to a boil. Add
the fish and reduce the heat to low. Cover and
cook for 10 minutes or until the fish flakes easily
when tested with a fork. Serve the fish with the
pineapple salsa.

Mediterranean Halibut with Couscous

START TO FINISH:
30 minutes

Prep: *15 minutes*
Cook: *15 minutes*

MAKES: **4 SERVINGS**

4 fresh halibut steaks, about 1-inch thick (about 1½ pounds)

¼ cup all-purpose flour

3 tablespoons olive oil

2 shallots, chopped

1 cup Swanson® Chicken Broth (Regular, Natural Goodness™ **or** Certified Organic)

2 teaspoons dried oregano leaves, crushed

1 can (14½ ounces) diced tomatoes, drained

½ cup kalamata olives, pitted and sliced

1 package (10 ounces) **uncooked** couscous (about 1½ cups)

Additional Swanson® Chicken Broth (Regular, Natural Goodness™ **or** Certified Organic)

1. Coat the fish with the flour.

2. Heat **2 tablespoons** of the oil in a 12-inch skillet over medium-high heat. Add the fish and cook for 8 minutes or until it's browned on both sides and flakes easily when tested with a fork. Remove the fish and keep it warm.

3. Reduce the heat to medium and add the remaining oil. Add the shallots and cook for 1 minute. Stir in the broth, oregano, tomatoes and olives. Heat to a boil. Cook for 5 minutes or until the sauce thickens slightly. Season to taste.

4. Prepare the couscous using broth instead of water according to the package directions. Spoon the couscous on a serving platter. Top with the fish. Spoon the sauce mixture over the fish.

Meatless
MEALS
&SIDES

RECIPES THAT MAKE A VEGETARIAN STATEMENT

Swiss Vegetable Bake

MAKES: **8 SERVINGS**

START TO FINISH:
50 minutes

Prep: *5 minutes*

Bake: *45 minutes*

Time-Saving Tip:
To thaw the vegetables, cut off 1 corner on bag, microwave on HIGH for 5 minutes.

1 can (26 ounces) Campbell's® Condensed Cream of Chicken Soup
⅔ cup sour cream
½ teaspoon ground black pepper
2 bags (16 ounces **each**) frozen vegetable combination (broccoli, cauliflower, carrots), thawed
2 cups shredded Swiss cheese (8 ounces)
1 can (6 ounces) French fried onions (2⅔ cups)

1. Stir the soup, sour cream, black pepper, vegetables, 1½ **cups** cheese and 1⅓ **cups** onions in a 13×9×2-inch shallow baking dish. Cover the dish with foil.

2. Bake at 350°F. for 40 minutes or until the vegetables are tender. Stir the vegetable mixture.

3. Sprinkle the remaining cheese and onions over the vegetable mixture. Bake for 5 minutes more or until the onions are golden brown.

Pasta Primavera

START TO FINISH:
25 minutes

Prep/Cook: *25 minutes*

3 cups **uncooked** corkscrew-shaped pasta
1 bag (16 ounces) frozen vegetable
    combination (broccoli, cauliflower, carrots)
1 jar (1 pound 10 ounces) Prego® Traditional
    Italian Sauce
    Grated Parmesan cheese

1. Prepare the pasta according to the package directions. Add the vegetables during the last 5 minutes of the cooking time. Drain the pasta and vegetables well in a colander.

2. Heat the Italian sauce in the same saucepot over medium heat. Add the pasta and vegetables and toss to coat with the sauce. Top with the cheese.

2-Step Nacho Pasta

MAKES: **4 SERVINGS**

START TO FINISH:
20 minutes

Prep/Cook: *20 minutes*

1 can (11 ounces) Campbell's® Condensed Fiesta Nacho Cheese Soup
½ cup milk
4 cups corkscrew-shaped pasta, cooked and drained

1. Heat the soup and milk in a 2-quart saucepan over medium heat. Cook until hot and bubbling.

2. Stir in the pasta. Cook and stir until hot.

Green Bean Casserole

MAKES: **6 SERVINGS**

Campbell's Kitchen Tip:
You can also make this classic side dish with fresh or canned green beans. You will need either 1½ pounds fresh green beans, cut into 1-inch pieces, cooked and drained **or** 2 cans (about 16 ounces **each**) cut green beans, drained for the frozen green beans.

1 can (10¾ ounces) Campbell's® Condensed Cream of Mushroom Soup (Regular **or** 98% Fat Free)
½ cup milk
1 teaspoon soy sauce
   Dash ground black pepper
2 packages (10 ounces **each**) frozen cut green beans, cooked and drained
1 can (2.8 ounces) French fried onions (1⅓ cups)

1. Stir the soup, milk, soy, black pepper, green beans and ⅔ **cup** onions in a 1½-quart casserole.

2. Bake at 350°F. for 25 minutes or until hot. Stir the green bean mixture.

3. Sprinkle the remaining onions over the green bean mixture. Bake for 5 minutes more or until onions are golden brown.

Broccoli and Pasta Bianco

MAKES: **8 SERVINGS**

START TO FINISH:
45 minutes

Prep: *20 minutes*

Bake: *25 minutes*

- 1 package (16 ounces) **uncooked** tube-shaped pasta (penne)
- 4 cups fresh **or** frozen broccoli flowerets
- 1 can (10¾ ounces) Campbell's® Condensed Cream of Mushroom Soup (Regular **or** 98% Fat Free)
- 1½ cups milk
- ½ teaspoon ground black pepper
- 1½ cups shredded mozzarella cheese (6 ounces)
- ¼ cup shredded Parmesan cheese

1. Prepare the pasta according to the package directions. Add the broccoli during the last 4 minutes of the cooking time. Drain the pasta and broccoli well in a colander.

2. Stir the soup, milk and black pepper in a 12×8 x 2-inch shallow baking dish. Stir in the pasta mixture, ¾ **cup** of the mozzarella cheese and **2 tablespoons** of the Parmesan cheese. Top with the remaining mozzarella and Parmesan cheeses.

3. Bake at 350°F. for 25 minutes or until hot and the cheese melts.

Golden Onions & Spinach Bake

MAKES: **8 SERVINGS**

1 can (10¾ ounces) Campbell's® Condensed Cream of Celery Soup (Regular **or** 98% Fat Free)
¼ cup sour cream
2 tablespoons grated Parmesan cheese
¼ teaspoon ground nutmeg
2 packages (about 10 ounces **each**) frozen chopped spinach, thawed and drained
1 can (2.8 ounces) French fried onions (1⅓ cups)

START TO FINISH:
30 minutes

Prep: *5 minutes*
Bake: *25 minutes*

Time-Saving Tip:
To thaw the spinach, microwave on HIGH for 3 minutes, breaking apart with a fork halfway through heating.

1. Stir the soup, sour cream, cheese, nutmeg, spinach and ⅔ **cup** of the onions in a 1½-quart casserole. Cover the dish with foil.

2. Bake at 350°F. for 20 minutes or until hot. Stir the spinach mixture.

3. Sprinkle the remaining onions over the spinach mixture. Bake for 5 minutes more or until the onions are golden brown.

Three Cheese Baked Ziti with Spinach

MAKES: **6 SERVINGS**

- 1 package (16 ounces) medium tube-shaped pasta (ziti)
- 1 bag (6 ounces) baby spinach leaves (4 cups), washed
- 1 jar (1 pound 9 ounces) Prego® Marinara Italian Sauce
- 1 cup ricotta cheese
- 1 cup shredded mozzarella cheese (4 ounces)
- ¾ cup grated Parmesan cheese
- ½ teaspoon garlic powder
- ¼ teaspoon ground black pepper

Campbell's Kitchen Tip:
Keep disposable aluminum foil baking pans on hand for convenience to tote casseroles to friends' parties or covered dish suppers. As a safety reminder, be sure to support the bottom of the filled pan when handling them in and out of the oven.

1. Prepare the pasta according to the package directions. Add the spinach during the last minute of the cooking time. Drain the pasta and spinach well in a colander. Return them to the saucepot.

2. Stir the Italian sauce, ricotta, ½ **cup** of the mozzarella cheese, ½ **cup** of the Parmesan cheese, garlic powder and black pepper into the saucepot. Spoon the pasta mixture into a 13×9×2-inch shallow baking dish. Sprinkle with the remaining mozzarella and Parmesan cheeses.

Make Ahead Tip:
Prepare through step 2. Cover and refrigerate up to 6 hours. Uncover and let come to room temperature before baking.

3. Bake at 350°F. for 30 minutes or until hot and bubbly.

Ratatouille with Penne

MAKES: **4 SERVINGS**

START TO FINISH:
*5½ to 6 hours,
15 minutes*

Prep: *15 minutes*
Bake: *5½ to 6 hours*

1   can (10¾ ounces) Campbell's® Condensed Tomato Soup
1   tablespoon olive oil
⅛ teaspoon ground black pepper
1   small eggplant, peeled and cut into ½-inch cubes (about 5 cups)
1   medium zucchini, thinly sliced (about 1½ cups)
1   medium red pepper, diced (about 1 cup)
1   large onion, sliced (about 1 cup)
1   clove garlic, minced
     Hot cooked tube-shaped pasta (penne)
     Grated Parmesan cheese (optional)

1. Heat the soup, olive oil, black pepper, eggplant, zucchini, red pepper, onion and garlic in a 4- to 5½-quart slow cooker.

2. Cover and cook on LOW for 5½ to 6 hours* or until the vegetables are tender.

3. Serve over the pasta. Serve with cheese, if desired.

Or on HIGH for 2½ to 3 hours

Hearty Bean & Barley Soup

MAKES: **6 SERVINGS**

START TO FINISH:
55 minutes

Prep: *15 minutes*
Cook: *40 minutes*

    1 tablespoon olive oil
    2 large carrots, coarsely chopped (about
        1 cup)
    2 stalks celery, sliced (about 1 cup)
    1 large onion, chopped (about 1 cup)
    3 cloves garlic, minced
3½ cups Swanson® Vegetable Broth (Regular
        or Certified Organic)
    1 can (about 15 ounces) red kidney beans,
        rinsed and drained
    1 can (14½ ounces) diced tomatoes
   ¼ cup **uncooked** pearl barley
    2 cups firmly packed chopped fresh spinach
        leaves
        Ground black pepper

1. Heat the oil in a 4-quart saucepan over medium-high heat. Add the carrots, celery, onion and garlic. Cook and stir until the vegetables are tender.

2. Stir the broth, beans, tomatoes and barley into the saucepan. Heat to a boil. Reduce the heat to low. Cover and cook for 30 minutes or until the barley is done.

3. Stir in the spinach and season to taste with black pepper.

Meatless
MEALS
*&*SIDES

West African Vegetable Stew

START TO FINISH:
45 minutes

Prep: *15 minutes*
Cook: *30 minutes*

MAKES: **6 SERVINGS**

1 tablespoon vegetable oil
2 cups sliced onions
2 cloves garlic, minced
2 sweet potatoes (about 1½ pounds), peeled and cut in half lengthwise and sliced
1 large tomato, coarsely chopped (1½ cups)
1 can (10½ ounces) Campbell's® Condensed Chicken Broth
½ cup water
½ teaspoon **each** ground cinnamon **and** crushed red pepper
½ cup raisins
4 cups coarsely chopped fresh spinach leaves
1 can (about 15 ounces) chickpeas (garbanzo beans), rinsed and drained
   Hot cooked rice **or** couscous (optional)

1. Heat the oil in a 4-quart saucepan over medium heat. Add the onions and garlic and cook until the onion is tender.

2. Add the potatoes and tomato. Cook and stir for 5 minutes.

3. Stir the broth, water, cinnamon, red pepper and raisins into the saucepan. Heat to a boil. Reduce the heat to low. Cover and cook for 15 minutes.

4. Stir in the spinach and chickpeas. Cook until hot. Serve over rice or couscous, if desired.

Meatless
MEALS
&SIDES

Hearty Vegetarian Chili

MAKES: **4 SERVINGS**

START TO FINISH:
30 minutes

Prep: *10 minutes*

Bake: *20 minutes*

Leftover Tip:
Reheat leftover chili and serve as a topping for baked potatoes.

1 tablespoon vegetable oil

1 large onion, chopped (about 1 cup)

1 large green pepper, chopped (about 1 cup)

1 tablespoon chili powder

1½ teaspoon ground cumin

¼ teaspoon garlic powder **or** 2 cloves garlic, minced

2½ cups V8® 100% Vegetable Juice

1 can (about 15 ounces) black **or** kidney beans, rinsed and drained

1 can (about 15 ounces) pinto beans, rinsed and drained

1. Heat the oil in a 6-quart saucepot over medium heat. Add the onion, pepper, chili powder, cumin and garlic powder. Cook and stir until the vegetables are tender.

2. Stir the vegetable juice into the saucepot. Heat to a boil. Reduce the heat to low. Cook for 5 minutes.

3. Stir in the beans. Cook until hot.

Toasted Corn & Sage Harvest Risotto

MAKES: **16 SERVINGS**

START TO FINISH:
50 minutes

Prep: *15 minutes*

Cook: *35 minutes*

- 1 tablespoon olive oil
- 1 cup fresh **or** drained, canned whole kernel corn
- 1 large orange **or** red pepper, chopped (about 1 cup)
- 1 medium onion, chopped (about ½ cup)
- 1¾ cups **uncooked** regular long-grain white rice
- 4 cups Swanson® Chicken Broth (Regular, Natural Goodness™ **or** Certified Organic)
- 1 teaspoon ground sage
- 1 can (10¾ ounces) Campbell's® Condensed Cream of Celery Soup (Regular **or** 98% Fat Free)
- ¼ cup grated Parmesan cheese

Campbell's Kitchen Tip:
If you want a meatless side dish, substitute Swanson® Vegetable Broth (Regular **or** Certified Organic)

1. Heat the oil in a 4-quart saucepan over medium heat. Add the corn, pepper and onion and cook for 6 minutes or until the vegetables start to brown. Add the rice and cook for 30 seconds, stirring constantly.

2. Stir the broth and sage into the saucepan. Heat to a boil. Reduce the heat to low. Cover the saucepan and cook for 20 minutes or until the rice is done and most of the liquid is absorbed.

3. Stir in the soup. Cook and stir for 2 minutes more or until hot. Sprinkle with the cheese.

Southwestern Bean Medley

MAKES: **8 SERVINGS**

Serving Suggestion Tip:
For a complete meal,
serve over hot cooked
rice.

1¾ cups Swanson® Vegetable Broth (Regular **or** Certified Organic)
1 tablespoon chili powder
1 teaspoon ground cumin
1 can (about 15 ounces **each**) black beans, chickpeas (garbanzo beans) **and** white kidney (cannellini) beans, rinsed and drained
½ cup dried lentils
1 can (14½ ounces) diced tomatoes and green chilies
Chopped fresh cilantro leaves

1. Stir the broth, chili powder, cumin, black beans, chickpeas, white kidney beans and lentils in a 3½-quart slow cooker.

2. Cover and cook on LOW for 6 to 7 hours*.

3. Stir in the tomatoes. Cover and cook for 1 hour more. Sprinkle with the cilantro.

Or on HIGH for 4 to 5 hours

Meatless
MEALS
& SIDES

Vegetable Stuffing Bake

MAKES: **6 SERVINGS**

START TO FINISH:
50 minutes

Prep: *15 minutes*

Bake: *35 minutes*

4 cups Pepperidge Farm® Herb Seasoned Stuffing

2 tablespoons butter, melted

1 can (10¾ ounces) Campbell's® Condensed Cream of Mushroom Soup (Regular **or** 98% Fat Free)

½ cup sour cream

2 small zucchini, shredded (about 2 cups)

2 medium carrots, shredded (about 1 cup)

1 small onion, finely chopped (about ¼ cup)

1. Stir **1 cup** of the stuffing and butter in a small bowl. Set the mixture aside.

2. Stir the soup, sour cream, zucchini, carrots and onion in a 1½-quart shallow baking dish. Add remaining stuffing and stir lightly to coat. Sprinkle with the reserved stuffing mixture.

3. Bake at 350°F. for 35 minutes or until hot.

Meatless
MEALS
*&*SIDES

Mostaccioli with Broccoli Rabe

MAKES: **8 SERVINGS**

START TO FINISH:
25 minutes

Prep: *10 minutes*

Cook: *15 minutes*

2 tablespoons olive oil

1 pound broccoli rabe, trimmed and cut into 1½-inch pieces (about 5 cups)

2 cloves garlic, minced

1¾ cups Swanson® Chicken Broth (Regular, Natural Goodness™ **or** Certified Organic)

1 jar (11 ounces) roasted red peppers, drained and chopped (about 1 cup)

¼ cup fresh basil leaves, cut into thin strips

1 package (16 ounces) medium tube-shaped pasta (mostaccioli), cooked and drained
   Grated Parmesan cheese

Campbell's Kitchen Tip:
Mostaccioli is a medium-size, tube-shaped pasta. This type of short good pasta is also known by other names such as ziti, ready-cut, mostaccioli, rigati or cut ziti.

1. Heat the oil in a 10-inch skillet over medium-high heat. Add the broccoli rabe and garlic and cook until the broccoli rabe is tender-crisp.

2. Stir the broth, peppers and basil into the skillet. Heat to a boil. Reduce the heat to low. Cover and cook for 10 minutes or until the broccoli rabe is tender, stirring occasionally.

3. Place the pasta in a large serving bowl. Add the broccoli rabe mixture and toss to coat. Serve with the cheese.

Index

Index

Index

Index

METRIC CONVERSION CHART

VOLUME MEASUREMENTS (dry)

$^1/_8$ teaspoon = 0.5 mL
$^1/_4$ teaspoon = 1 mL
$^1/_2$ teaspoon = 2 mL
$^3/_4$ teaspoon = 4 mL
1 teaspoon = 5 mL
1 tablespoon = 15 mL
2 tablespoons = 30 mL
$^1/_4$ cup = 60 mL
$^1/_3$ cup = 75 mL
$^1/_2$ cup = 125 mL
$^2/_3$ cup = 150 mL
$^3/_4$ cup = 175 mL
1 cup = 250 mL
2 cups = 1 pint = 500 mL
3 cups = 750 mL
4 cups = 1 quart = 1 L

VOLUME MEASUREMENTS (fluid)

1 fluid ounce (2 tablespoons) = 30 mL
4 fluid ounces ($^1/_2$ cup) = 125 mL
8 fluid ounces (1 cup) = 250 mL
12 fluid ounces (1$^1/_2$ cups) = 375 mL
16 fluid ounces (2 cups) = 500 mL

WEIGHTS (mass)

$^1/_2$ ounce = 15 g
1 ounce = 30 g
3 ounces = 90 g
4 ounces = 120 g
8 ounces = 225 g
10 ounces = 285 g
12 ounces = 360 g
16 ounces = 1 pound = 450 g

DIMENSIONS

$^1/_{16}$ inch = 2 mm
$^1/_8$ inch = 3 mm
$^1/_4$ inch = 6 mm
$^1/_2$ inch = 1.5 cm
$^3/_4$ inch = 2 cm
1 inch = 2.5 cm

OVEN TEMPERATURES

250°F = 120°C
275°F = 140°C
300°F = 150°C
325°F = 160°C
350°F = 180°C
375°F = 190°C
400°F = 200°C
425°F = 220°C
450°F = 230°C

BAKING PAN AND DISH EQUIVALENTS

Utensil	Size in Inches	Size in Centimeters	Volume	Metric Volume
Baking or Cake Pan (square or rectangular)	8×8×2	20×20×5	8 cups	2 L
	9×9×2	23×23×5	10 cups	2.5 L
	13×9×2	33×23×5	12 cups	3 L
Loaf Pan	8½×4½×2½	21×11×6	6 cups	1.5 L
	9×9×3	23×13×7	8 cups	2 L
Round Layer Cake Pan	8×1½	20×4	4 cups	1 L
	9×1½	23×4	5 cups	1.25 L
Pie Plate	8×1½	20×4	4 cups	1 L
	9×1½	23×4	5 cups	1.25 L
Baking Dish or Casserole			1 quart/4 cups	1 L
			1½ quart/6 cups	1.5 L
			2 quart/8 cups	2 L
			3 quart/12 cups	3 L